Vacation Crafts

Books by Phyllis Méras

First Spring: A Martha's Vineyard Journal
A Yankee Way with Wood
Miniatures: How to Make Them, Use Them, Sell Them
Vacation Crafts

Phyllis Méras

Vacation Crafts

Houghton Mifflin Company
Boston 1978

Photographs by the author unless noted
Drawings by Jane Tenenbaum

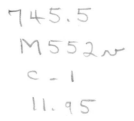

Library of Congress Cataloging in Publication Data

Méras, Phyllis.   Vacation crafts.

1. Handicraft.   2. Nature craft.   I. Title.
TT157.M458   745.5   78-2774
          ISBN 0-395-26498-7

Printed in the United States of America

A 10 9 8 7 6 5 4 3 2 1

To H.B.H.
Who opened the way

Acknowledgments

Craftspeople from all over the country have generously contributed their time, their ideas, and their creations to the preparation of this book. I am especially grateful to Marshall Lockhart, Ruth Nerney, Virginia Smith, and Bettyanne Twigg for their many suggestions and for their unflagging willingness to assist in the revising of this material.

Also helpful have been Amyas Ames, Jacqueline Andrews, Eileen Argenziano, Georgia Bailey, Ursula Beau-Seigneur, Ann Billings, Blaine Blackburn of the Rag Doll Craft Shop in Flat Rock, North Carolina, Doyle Blalock, Shirley Blau, Sophie Block, Ruth Bogan, Alma Briggs of the Roc Shop in Edgartown, Massachusetts, Del Brinkman, Florence Brown, Audrey Steiner Bugbee, Ernest and Irene Butler of Butler's Rock Shop in Lewiston, Idaho.

Anne Campbell, Mary Frances Carey, Carolyn Carter of the Georgia Bureau of Industry and Trade, Mara Cary, Marylin Chou, Clinton H. Cram, Edward Comstock of the Adirondack Museum, Blue Mountain Lake, New York, Richard Countryman of the Arizona Commission of Agriculture and Horticulture, David Dary, Lillian Diven of the Desert Botanical Garden of Arizona, Mariella Dumont, Sanford Evans, Pamela Freedman, Carol and Dick Gardner, James Gentry of the Southern Highlands Handicraft Guild, Ruth Gottlieb, May Harden, Tina Helm, Harry M. Hess, Jr., Channing Hilliard, Hatsie Hornblower, John T. Hughes of the Massachusetts State Lobster Hatchery, Louise Tate King, Robert Lawrence, Marion Lillie, Donal MacPhee, Alice Mathewson, Beth Meehan, Polly Woollcott Murphy, Eugene Nathan, Marianna O'Brien.

Mary Patton, Rita Price of the Roc Shop in Edgartown, Massachusetts, Domer Ridings of Callaway Gardens, Pine Mountain, Georgia, Roy Ross, Hildegarde Ruof, Sara Shepard, Wenonah Silva, Susan Sirkis, Dee Snyder, Pat Spiewack, Dorothy Stevens, Rose Treat, John C. Upton,

Shirley Utterback, Dr. John E. Wallace, Fran Weeren, Dona Welch of the Vermont Agency of Development and Community Affairs, Brandon Wight of Alan-Mayhew Ltd., Vineyard Haven, Massachusetts, Dr. Robert White, James Dugan and Leighton Authier of the Providence (R.I.) *Journal.*

For assistance in the taking, developing, and printing of pictures I am particularly indebted to Alison Shaw, but also to George Adams, David Balfour, Francisca Fred, Mark Lennihan, Robert McCrystal, Joan Noone, Thomas D. Stevens, and Henny Wenkart.

And for their patience while this book was in progress, to Thomas Cocroft, Fay and Henry Russell, and, above all, to Frances Tenenbaum.

Contents

Introduction

A silver bowl on my mantelpiece holds chunks of lava from the Azores, black and white stones from a Greek Island beach, and a handful of pink shells from Florida. Whenever my eyes fall on the bowl, I remember the temple of Poseidon outside of Athens and the beach below it where I found the stones, the soft Azorean twilight on Faial, and lazy beachcombing holidays in Florida.

Wheat from Kansas is framed on my bedroom wall, and my coffee table is Martha's Vineyard driftwood. When the sun comes in the window, the jar of beach glass in my kitchen sparkles as if it were stained glass.

Every vacation is rich in memories of dramatic headlands, sloping dunes, and lemon sunsets. But even the strongest memories fade without something tangible to keep them vivid, and this, of course, accounts for the existence of both the stores selling mainly gimcrack souvenirs and the cars that return from vacation trips loaded down with rocks and pine cones, pieces of driftwood or old barn shingles, shells and dried pods. The collecting tourist is both insatiable (a European friend of mine paid a considerable amount in overweight air fare to carry home her American pebbles) and optimistic; the truth is that most of the things we gather end up in boxes in the attic.

But they shouldn't, for we were right when we picked them up to believe we could make something of them (if we only knew how). Through crafts, it is possible to make the collectibles from your vacation into mementos that have meaning beyond the value of the piece itself. Vacation crafts can enhance a trip in many ways — not only will you find materials that are free for the taking, your eyes will be opened to fascinating aspects of the environment that you might never have noticed before. Not least important, most of the crafts in this book can be done by

11

children or by parents and children together. The things you collect on a sunny day at the beach will provide hours of pleasure on a rainy one. And for the vacation craftsmen there is extra solace in the bad weather, since storms wash up new treasures along lakes and seashores.

For years I have traveled both professionally and for pleasure, but only recently, as I have crisscrossed the country collecting material for craft books, have I become aware of the infinite and fascinating variety of objects that can be made of materials indigenous to an area or a terrain. From craftspeople and talented tourists I have learned how to make birds and animals from pods and cones and even rocks; how to make my own paper and natural dyes from the plants that grow along country roads; how to make brass rubbings in a church or tombstone rubbings in a country cemetery; how to make sand paintings and seaweed pudding; baskets from pine needles or honeysuckle; jewelry from beach stones and Arizona cholla plants; a barn-board clock; dolls from seashells, apples, corn husks, and even a lobster. Christmas wreaths and decorations made from the collectibles of summer have a special significance.

Vacations are all too fleeting. No souvenir you buy in a shop can provide as much pleasure as the ones you make yourself.

Vacation Crafts

1
Wood
From seashore, forest, farm, and desert

Ordinarily, the vacationer looks forward to bright, sunshiny days for beaching and boating and picnicking, but if a morning arrives at a lake or seaside resort when the sky is lowering and the wind blows hard, there can be compensations. Not only is a rainy day ideal for settling down at the kitchen table with already collected memorabilia of a holiday and fashioning them into long-lasting remembrances, but if you have an adventurous spirit, don a slicker — it's a fine time for beachcombing.

Ship's timbers, lobster pots and buoys, hatchcovers, and gnarled tree limbs are often carried by the high storm tide into coves and nooks among the rocks and dunes and are there for the taking. With a little artistry, mysterious, weathered old ship's timbers can become coffee tables, picture frames, and garden sculpture.

If your vacation is on a lake, the same hunting advice holds true. After a storm, the beaches of the Great Lakes are covered with driftwood. Inland vacationers will also find weathered roots and wood if they follow streambeds. Here, too, the hunting is better after a downpour.

The wood of desert cactus skeletons can be found regardless of the weather. But the traveler seeking it should check on state plant protection laws.

And down on the farm, the wood of barn boards, old fences, and shingles lends itself to memories in the form of frames and mountings. The woodland walker anywhere may find gnarled sticks for canes — tree limbs left behind from a lumbering operation or trees cut and abandoned where the woods have been thinned. These, too, may be lugged home to evoke memories.

Because fresh water does not whiten wood the way salt water does, you may wish to color and preserve freshwater driftwood with a coating of butcher's wax. This will give it a blond tone.

Writer-artist-beachcomber Yuri Suhl points out that the tools and craftsmanship required for driftwood sculpture are minimal. Weathered wood, he believes, should be allowed to tell its own story, so he uses only a few chisels, an electric drill, Titebond glue, and a hammer in his work. "Driftwood comes in its own shape or in the form to which nature shaped it. I am simply a collaborator with nature." Fence and bedposts, trellises, tree stumps, rudders, cheese boxes, doors, packing cases — all have been incorporated into the sculpture that adorns his Massachusetts garden.

Weathered driftwood boards are a Yuri Suhl bird sculpture. Bits of old paint feather the wings.

Flat pieces of driftwood or old shingles make a pretty background for a painting of a bird or flower or of the country cottage where you spent your vacation. To prepare driftwood or shingles for painting, dry them thoroughly. Coat them once with natural-colored Cuprinol and let them dry. Apply a second coat and let that dry before you start your painting. The Cuprinol will keep the paint from sinking into the wood. Sketch the design you wish and then paint with acrylics. Buy screw eyes and an attractive chain if you want to hang the painting from the wall.

Shingles and driftwood can also be prettily decorated with dried grasses or flowers, lichen, or shells (cotton should be glued into the shells, however, so they do not break too easily). Driftwood can also make a charmingly casual name sign to hang over your door.

Left: A Rakish Lady fashioned by Yuri Suhl from mooring line, an old garden rake, a lobster pot, barrel pieces, some net, and part of a baby's crib washed ashore. Right: Odds and ends of a lobster pot became this Lobster Maiden by Yuri Suhl.

Three driftwood owls perch on a driftwood tree.

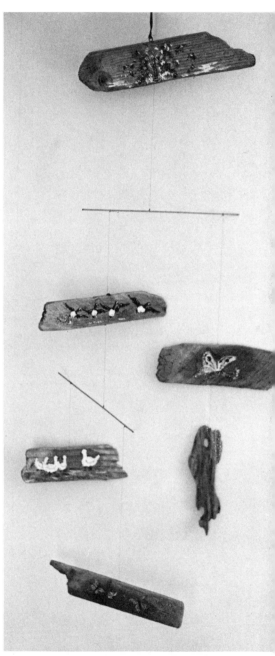

Claire Duys decorates driftwood with paintings of the swans that swim in the pond near her vacation home.

You can make a mobile from decorated driftwood pieces. This one was made by Claire Duys.

Above: Driftwood mementos need not be monumental in size. This nubbin of wood from the Great Lakes, painted with a touch of acrylic, has become a brooch.

Right: A smiling carving is a remembrance of Switzerland. (Alison Shaw)

Below: Skate's egg cases — mermaid's purses — found on a beach, are glued to a shingle for this Ballet Class by Louise Tate King.

Tall and short, fat and thin, are the shingle and driftwood members of this family tree. (Joan Noone)

Dried flowers on a shingle hang outside a country home.

Above: This driftwood fish swam into Rita Price's ken on Martha's Vineyard.

Above: A root from a woodland stream becomes a grotesque man. (Francisca Fred)

19

A wide-eyed stone critter looks over his driftwood terrain.

Waves of the Cape Cod shore designed this sculpture for the garden of Ted and Dolores Goodes.

Top left: A driftwood lamp fits well into a holiday décor.

Above: A stone owl enjoys a driftwood perch.

Left: A chunk of birch from a woodland walk becomes an attractive candleholder. (Alison Shaw)

21

Not infrequently, travelers in desolate areas of Vermont or Maine will happen upon tumbledown barns. An inquiry of a neighbor will generally establish if they are truly abandoned. Even if the wood looks wormeaten, it can be effectively used in picture frames. If there are nails in the wood, remove them with pliers. The nail holes will add to the rustic effect.

With a table saw, cut strips from the top and bottom of the board however wide you wish your frame to be. Stain the freshly cut side a shade

A fence board picture frame made by Eugene Nathan.

that will match the uncut part and let it dry. Cut four strips to make the sides for your frame. With your table saw or router, cut a rabbet into which you will fit your picture. Miter the ends of your strips so they will fit together neatly at the corners. Apply Titebond to the mitered edges. Clamp them together until they are thoroughly dry. For reinforcement, nail-set small finish nails in the corners and putty the holes with wood putty, or fasten the corners in back with Skotch wood joiners, No. 1.

A BARN-BOARD CLOCK

Peter Bettencourt of Edgartown, Massachusetts, used a Vermont barn board to fashion a clock instead of a picture frame. Here are his directions:

Materials

one 12 x 12-inch piece of barn board, 3/4 inch thick (for the clock face)
four strips of 12-inch-long, 2-inch-wide board (to edge the face)
one 2-inch wide, 12-inch-long strip of barn or other board (what this is doesn't matter, since it won't show)
Elmer's glue
4-penny finish nails or wire brads
square-headed nails pulled from a board or bought from the Tremont Nail Company in Wareham, Massachusetts
clock works

1. Pull all of the nails out of the barn board and save them.
2. With a table or hand saw cut the face board and edging strips.
3. With a miter box and hand saw, miter the edges of the strips so they will fit neatly together.
4. Glue the mitered corners with Elmer's glue and nail them together with finish nails or wire brads.
5. With more wire brads or nails, attach the edge to the face of the clock, allowing about 1/4-inch overhang on all sides to create a sense of depth.
6. Cut the nails so each is 3/8 inch long, excluding the head. Hammer them, flush, into the face of the clock at the hour points.
7. Drill a 3/4-inch hole in the center of the face for the clock shaft. Attach the works behind the face and the hands to the face.
8. To hang the clock, drill a hole large enough to insert a nail head in the center of the 2-inch-wide strip. Cut it to fit across the back of the clock and nail it in place about 1 inch from the top of the back of the clock.

A Vermont barn board found on a country holiday can be turned into an attractive clock.

COASTERS

A limb about 3 inches in diameter, cut at an angle with a hand saw to about 1/2 inch thick, will make attractive coasters. If the wood is old and the bark begins to fall off, glue it back on with clear 5-minute epoxy. Sand. Then with a small gouge, carve a decoration in the top so the sweat from the glass will have someplace to run. (Otherwise, the glass will stick to the coaster.) Sand again. Slop on mineral oil until the wood will no longer absorb it. Wipe off the excess. Check your coaster to be sure that it is even across the bottom or the glass put on it will slide. Sand until it is even.

A rustic coaster like this one by R. Dennis Cutler starts with a half-inch-thick slice of tree limb.

A RUSTIC PLATTER

If you spend your holiday in the woods, you may well end up near a lumbering camp. If so, ask if there is a white oak or maple or yellow birch log — or the stump of one — being left behind. An 8-to-10-inch long log can be transformed into a useful platter. Robert Lawrence of Chilmark, Massachusetts, has made one of red oak that reminds him of a holiday he took on his family's New Jersey farm. However, woodcraftsman Jack Upton of Damariscotta, Maine, prefers white oak or maple or yellow birch for longevity's sake.

1. With a sledgehammer and wedges, split the log lengthwise into three parts. The inside piece, which should be 2 to 2 1/2 inches thick in its rough state, will become the platter.
2. First remove the bark with a draw shave. (It is, of course, possible to leave it on for a rustic effect. If you do this, nail it on with 16- or 18-gauge brads. With the bark on it, remember in cleaning it, however, not to soak it in water, but simply to wipe it clean after use. And you may, in time, have to glue the bark on with waterproof glue, for, as it ages, it will start to fall off.)

25

3. With a hand plane, set first for a coarse cut, then for a fine cut, smooth the two sides of the slab. Then sand them with No. 80 sandpaper, followed by No. 100 and then by No. 120. Use a rotary motion with the No. 120 so that you are sure to erase all the scratches the coarser paper has made.
4. Next, with a No. 3 coarse bent gouge, make a sinking about 3 inches in diameter, 3/8 inch deep, to catch the juices. Run a channel around the outside of the stock using the same gouge about 3/8 inch in from the edge.
5. Coat the platter with vegetable oil and wipe off.

MINIATURE BIRCHBARK CANOE

Sometimes in the North Woods you may find broken-off white birch limbs or a white birch toppled by a storm. If so, there is no reason not to peel off a bit of the bark (which is probably peeling off anyway) to make into a miniature birchbark canoe. (Bark should never be peeled from a living tree, of course, since the birch cannot survive without its protection.) White birchbark is made up of very thin layers. If the outside of the piece you want is dirty, usually you can peel the top layer off.

Charles H. Spilman, who makes little canoes for his grandchildren to remember their New England holiday by, gives his directions:

1. Get a large piece of bark that is only three or four or five layers thick, one thin enough to be quite flexible. You will need a smaller piece a little thicker, and a still thicker piece — about 3/32 or 1/8 inch thick — that has many layers and is quite stiff.
2. Make a paper pattern. Draw an outline of one side of the canoe as you want it to be, using whatever dimensions are pleasing. The bow and stern can sweep up high or be quite stubby, or the bow can be high and the stern low — whatever you want. Just remember that when you pull the ends together the sides will bulge out slightly, so on your pattern the distance from the bottom of the boat to the top of the side should be somewhat higher than it will be in the finished boat (Pattern A).
3. Trace the outline of the profile on another piece of paper. Then flip the profile over, keel to keel, and trace a mirror outline (A and B). Cut this double outline out of your thin sheet of birchbark *in one piece*. Then bring the ends together and glue them. You can use any kind of glue, household cement or carpenter's glue. Contact cement may be

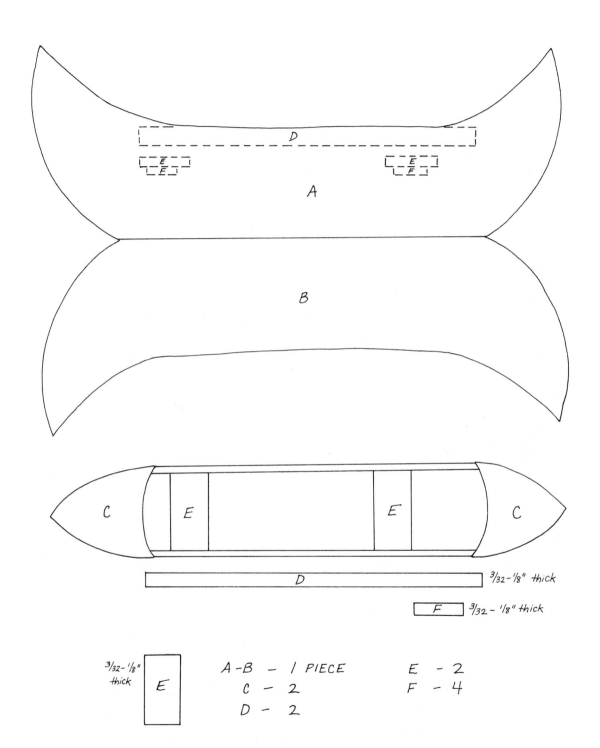

A

B

C E E C

D $^3/_{32}$-$^1/_8$" thick

F $^3/_{32}$ - $^1/_8$" thick

$^3/_{32}$-$^1/_8$"
thick   E

A-B — 1 PIECE   E - 2
C - 2   F - 4
D - 2

easier, because once the parts are put together there is no need to clamp them or squeeze them for a time, although they have to be put together right the first time, as they can't be moved.

4. If you don't like the sheer, or curve, of the bow when you have glued it, you can alter it a little with scissors, but you can't cut beyond the limit of the glued area.

5. Cut out two pieces from the heavier bark to make the gunwales (Part D). The dimensions aren't too critical. The piece should be thicker than the shell of the boat but flexible enough to bend with the side. Glue the pieces along the inside of the shell, flush with the upper edge. If the match isn't exact, the line of the gunwale can be trimmed with a sharp knife after the glue has hardened.

6. Add the decking in the ends, if you want. (Or you can leave the ends open.) If you use it, cut from thin pieces of bark two sections (Pattern C) that conform to the flare of the sides. Fitting these can be tricky, so make sure they're in just right before you apply the glue.

7. Cut four small pieces of heavy stuff (Pattern F) to support the thwarts, or seats (Pattern E), which also are to be taken from bark thick enough to make them stiff. Glue the support pieces to the inside of the boat, positioning them so that the afterthwart is nearer the stern than the forward is near the bow. When the glue has dried, glue the thwarts on top of them. The thwarts should be whatever width you decide is proper for the proportions of the canoe. Determine their length from the boat itself and fit each one separately, for the flare of the sides may make each one slightly different.

That's all there is to it.

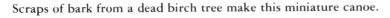

Scraps of bark from a dead birch tree make this miniature canoe.

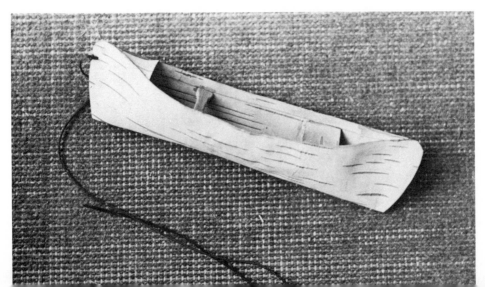

From wood collected on his travels, Bob Wells of Pigeon Forge, Tennessee, has carved these walking sticks.

WALKING STICKS

A true vacation craftsman is Bob Wells of Pigeon Forge, Tennessee, who has a set of walking sticks he has carved from the state trees of almost every state. On the top of each, he has fashioned either the state bird or animal. A member of the National Campers and Hikers Association, he conceived his walking stick idea in 1970 on a camping trip. The first walking stick he carved was made from a sweet gum tree and had a pileated woodpecker sitting on the side. His West Virginia walking stick is maple with a black bear on the handle. The Arkansas walking stick is cedar with a razorback decoration. The Tennessee stick — since Tennessee is his natal state — is more richly carved than the rest. A raccoon, a Tennessee walking horse, and a mockingbird — the state bird — are all in relief on his tulip tree cane.

Mr. Wells's wood is generally green when he picks it, on hillsides and along streambeds. Sometimes he uses roots, sometimes limbs. He keeps the wood in the shade to season, perhaps for just a few weeks, perhaps for several years, depending on the condition of the wood and his own inclination. He advises cutting the wood for canes in winter when the sap is down.

Cypress Knees

If you travel in Georgia or Florida, you are sure to see cypress knees being sold by the roadside, and if you venture into the swamps with a guide, you will find them growing. A good way of finding a guide, according to Tennessean George Lockhart, is simply to go to a general store and ask the storekeeper to refer you to one. Once you have a guide, tell him you are eager to have a cypress stump to remember your expedition by. You will need a saw to remove the tree, so be sure to mention your interest in advance.

When you have your knee, dry it out, for it will be full of water. You can even drill a small hole in it to get the water out. Then study it to see what shape it suggests to you. Each cypress knee has a character of its own that you can easily develop. The wood is fibrous, but easy to carve, and very little sanding is necessary. Cypress knees can make bookends or table bases or mantelpiece sculpture. When your piece is done, wax it with furniture paste wax.

Once this was a Florida cypress knee, but George Lockhart took it home to Tennessee and saw these figures in it.

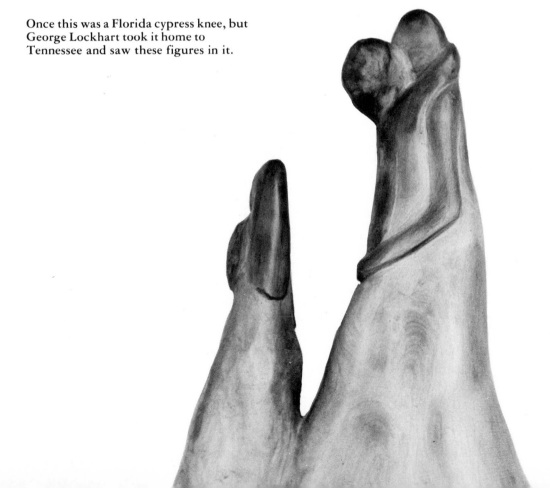

Another woodland art that calls for imagination — seeing the shape already in it rather than carving a shape — is lightwood sculpture. When a pitch pine tree rots, rosin concentrates in the heart of the junction of the limb, and a prettily marked wood — called lightwood — is created. If you break off the dead wood around the lightwood and find an interesting shape, sand it smooth with wet and dry sandpaper of medium grit. If the shape lends itself to a vase, bore a hole in it 1 inch in diameter about 2 inches deep with a bit and bitstock. Then clean out the hole and dip the vase in clear lacquer, or spray it with lacquer and let it dry. This vase is good for dried weeds or flowers, but not for those that require water.

George Lockhart also makes pendants and earrings from lightwood. With a band saw, he saws the wood into 1/8-inch slices, sands them with wet and dry sandpaper of medium grit; bores a hole in one end (through which to string a thong or chain), and dips them into a clear spray-type lacquer. Since there is so much rosin in lightwood, be sure to clean your saw blades and sandpaper with solvent carefully after using them.

Lightwood from the heart of a pitch pine tree can be a host of mementos.

31

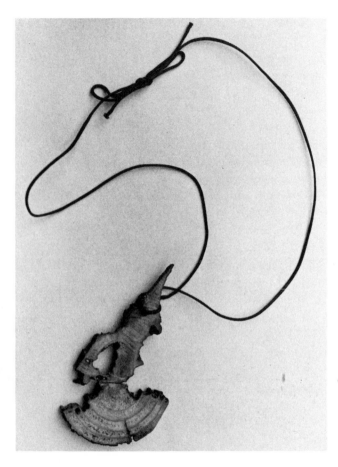

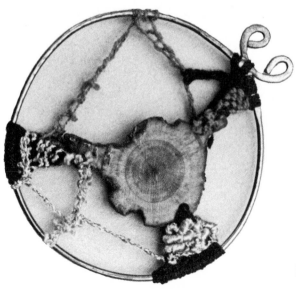

Top left: A Balinese dancer pendant cut from a piece of lightwood.

Top right: Lightwood makes a pretty weed pot.

Left: Lightwood and stitchery are combined to make this pendant.

Wood isn't found only on beaches and in forests. Cactus skeletons are wood, too, and although gathering living cactus from the desert is frowned upon — the minimum fine for removing living cactus from either public or private property in Arizona without a permit is $100, the maximum a year in jail, or both — the skeletons of both saguaro and cholla may be used, as long as they are not taken from government property. (Only 17 percent of Arizona is private property, however.) Saguaro ribs make walking sticks and picture frames as well as planters and little tables for plants. But they do have thorns on them, so wear gloves when you scrape them off. A beer can opener is an effective scraping tool.

Below: A Southwest arrangement is made of prickly pear cactus pads, a cholla cactus skeleton, and desert rocks. (Desert Botanical Garden)

More adaptable to household use is the lacelike cholla skeleton. Saw the piece you have picked up into the right size for a planter. Clean out the dead matter inside (it resembles gray shredded wheat). Attach it to a base of desert driftwood, or simply put a plant into it as is. Some people also make lamps of the skeleton. Beads for decorating macramé and tie slides for neckerchiefs may also be cut from it. Cholla can either be used as is or coated with clear lacquer.

In the desert there is also ironwood, almost like ebony in its handsomeness, and mesquite, which, Arizonans say, imparts a very special flavor to charcoal-broiled steaks.

In higher desert elevations there is manzanita, and its reddish-brown bark is often used in planters. Like the cactus, manzanita should not be cut or removed without written permission from the owner and a permit from the Arizona Commission of Agriculture and Horticulture, which costs $1.

Left: A holiday in Mexico is recalled in this cactus skeleton arrangement by Mrs. L. B. Lindemuth of Chagrin Falls, Ohio. (Joan Noone) Right: Travel in the tropics and the desert resulted in this artistic arrangement of driftwood, fan coral, and cactus.

2

Cones, nuts, and pods

Souvenir craft materials from the woods need not be wood. There are so many flowers and leaves to be pressed, wild fruits to preserve, nuts and cones and seeds to transform into dining room centerpieces, holiday wreaths, wall plaques, jewelry, and mobiles.

BIRDS AND ANIMALS

Dorothy Tresner, who lives in Asheville, North Carolina, has been a woodland walker for years. In the summer she goes to neighboring Georgia to instruct vacationers how to remember their holidays by handcrafting souvenirs from nature.

Many of her creations are birds and animals made from the cones, nuts, burrs, and pods of the South. Of course, you can substitute the materials of your own vacation woods for the ones in her directions. Be sure, though, to put your nuts or cones in a 150- to 200-degree oven for an hour to kill any bugs. It is best to gather cones from recently felled trees, preferably in the spring, when the cones are fresh and shiny. If they are old, spray them with a light coat of clear plastic spray before using them, or apply a very light coat of gesso with a watercolor brush and let it dry; then spray-paint them.

Cone rabbits   In autumn, when the beechnuts fall and their outer shells split, Mrs. Tresner uses them for the ears of spruce cone rabbits. Pussy willows make the feet, pussy willows or hare's tail grass the tails, papier-mâché (or Celluclay) combined with 1/4 teaspoon of dry brown tempera for every 2 level tablespoons of papier-mâché, is the head. Here are Mrs. Tresner's directions:

35

A family of spruce cone rabbits with pussy willow feet and beechnut shell ears.

1. To make a rabbit, wind a 3-inch piece of No. 30 soft, untempered steel wire under about the third scales from the base of a cone.
2. With a pair of needlenose pliers, twist the ends of the wire into a coil and mold about 1/4 teaspoon of the papier-mâché around it, shaping it into a rabbit head. Press it firmly against the flat end of the cone as you work.
3. Take pruning shears and cut the beechnut husks in two. (If you try to break them apart, they may split.) You should get two pairs of ears from each husk.
4. Put a little Elmer's glue or 3M Scotch Super Strong Adhesive on the end of each husk and insert the husks in the head in the appropriate spots for ears.
5. With the end of a paintbrush, make little eyeholes. Dab a bit of glue in the holes and insert pokeberry seeds or other shiny black seeds.
6. Glue on the feet and the tail.
7. Attach the rabbits to a circle of wood sawed from a fallen tree, or to a shingle or a piece of bark, either with glue or by drilling two 1/32-inch holes in the wood, taking a piece of No. 30 wire, fastening it under some of the cone scales, and making it into a U. Push the ends through the two drilled holes and twist the ends of the wire together under the wood. Press them flat.
8. To keep the wires from scratching your furniture, glue a piece of felt to the back of the wood with Elmer's.
9. Glue a little grass or a twig next to the rabbits for atmosphere.

The tiny mouse on the left side of the driftwood has a pussy willow body, a papier-mâché head, and eyes of cockscomb seeds.

Pussy willow mice   A mouse may easily be made with a pussy willow body, a tail of buttonhole thread glued in place with Elmer's or Scotch Super Strength Adhesive, and with coxcomb seeds for eyes, glued into a papier-mâché head.

Mrs. Tresner often glues her mice to a rounded black walnut shell from the woods. Sometimes she takes a 3/16-inch dowel, cut about 1/2 inch long, and inserts it into a 1/4-inch hole she drills in the shell. It resembles cheese.

Quail family   Hemlock cones from a trip to the Blue Ridge Mountains can be the basis for fine baby quail. The heads, again, are papier-mâché; the feet No. 28 wire twisted around and under the pine cone scales. The mother bird is a jack pine cone; her tail is a Norway spruce scale, and her wings are made from the outside of a cotton boll glued on with Elmer's or Scotch Super Strength Adhesive.

Mama quail is made of a jack pine cone; the babies are made of hemlock cones. You could substitute any cones of suitable size.

Mrs. Tresner suggests, "If you're visiting in Georgia or Alabama in the fall, ask a farmer if you can't have some of his cotton boll pods. He'll think you're crazy, but that's all right. They make nice mementos of a southern vacation. For wings, you want the flattest possible pods, and be sure they're dried out."

Attach the birds to whatever base you wish, with either glue or wire. To paint the birds' heads, use acrylics and follow the color pattern in a bird identification book.

Hummingbirds Hummingbirds, the way Mrs. Tresner fashions them, are made with a red spruce cone as the body and a painted papier-mâché head. The beak is a pin. (There is no need for feet.) The tail is a small Norway spruce cone scale or a small scale from a white pine cone. The wings are the inside membrane of the cotton boll. You can use maple wing seeds as a substitute.

First, collect some lichen for the nest. Glue or wire it to a piece of driftwood or a twig tree. If you don't like the color of the wood, bleach it by dropping it for a few minutes into a plastic or enamel bucket filled with equal parts of Clorox and water.

Make a papier-mâché "nest" by pressing it into a child's tiny teacup. Leave it overnight. In the morning, glue the lichen to the outside of the papier-mâché. Line the inside of the nest with milkweed pods or thistledown.

Hummingbird mobile To make a mobile, Mrs. Tresner uses three hummingbirds, two pieces of steel stitcher wire from a print shop, and nylon thread. Here's how to do it.

1. Cut one wire 5 inches long, the other 4 inches. On the ends of both wires, make loops by winding the wires around the end of a pair of needlenose pliers. Then, with nylon thread, attach a bird to each end of the shorter wire.
2. To the center of that wire, tie a 4- to 5-inch piece of nylon thread. At the end of the thread, tie one end of the longer wire.
3. Attach the third hummingbird to the other end of the longer wire. Exactly where on the thread the longer wire should be is determined by the weight of the hummingbird. Keep experimenting by moving the wire on the thread until the mobile is balanced.
4. When balance has been achieved, attach about 30 inches of nylon thread to the top of the mobile so you can hang it.

Left: A red spruce cone is the body of this hummingbird. Its beak is a pin. Right: Pine cones, milkweed pods, catalpa beans, and pokeberry seeds are the ingredients of this lifelike mourning dove.

MOURNING DOVE IN A BASKET

Materials

milkweed pod
catalpa bean
one yellow jack pine cone
No. 26 soft wire (for attaching the bird to its nest)
No. 30 soft wire (for attaching the bird's head to its body)
three teaspoons papier-mâché
Elmer's glue or Scotch Super Strength Adhesive
pokeberry seeds (for eyes)
acrylic paints
plumber's lead or drapery weights
straw or Spanish moss
small teacup
velvet ribbon

1. Split the milkweed pod in half. Each half will be used for one wing.
2. Cut a catalpa bean into three pieces for the bird's tail (the middle piece should be larger than the two side pieces).

3. Wrap the milkweed pod in a damp cloth and leave it in a plastic bag overnight so it will be pliable. If the catalpa bean is stubborn, put it in the same damp cloth as the wings.
4. Wind a 3-inch piece of the 30-gauge soft wire under about the third row of scales from the base of the cone. The head will be attached to this.
5. Wrap about 2 teaspoons of papier-mâché around the wire, shaping it into a dove head and pressing it firmly against the cone while shaping.
6. Wind a 6-inch piece of the 26-gauge wire around the middle scale of the cone. You will attach the bird to its nest with this.
7. Attach the milkweed pod wings and the catalpa tail with Elmer's or with Scotch Super Strength Adhesive.
8. Glue in the pokeberry seed eyes.
9. Paint with acrylics.
10. Model eggs out of papier-mâché. You will need 1/2 teaspoon for each egg. Doves usually lay only two eggs each year.
11. Insert plumber's lead or drapery weights into the basket so it will balance. (Practice by putting the bird on the edge of the basket, too.)
12. To make the nest, dilute Elmer's glue with water, half and half, and mix it with a handful of Spanish moss. Press the moss into a child's teacup and then let it dry overnight. In the morning, press it into the cup shape again if necessary.
13. Cut whatever length of ribbon you need and hang the nest.

A variety of pine cones combine to make this proud creature.

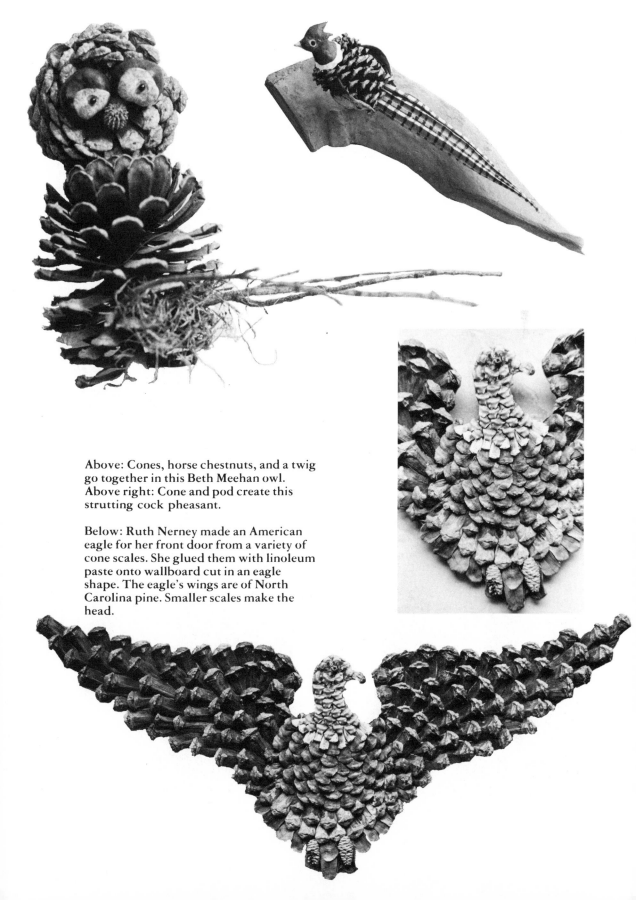

Above: Cones, horse chestnuts, and a twig go together in this Beth Meehan owl. Above right: Cone and pod create this strutting cock pheasant.

Below: Ruth Nerney made an American eagle for her front door from a variety of cone scales. She glued them with linoleum paste onto wallboard cut in an eagle shape. The eagle's wings are of North Carolina pine. Smaller scales make the head.

Right: From the deep woods comes this black walnut pair, glued to bark with Sobo. Below: Sliced hickory nuts, black walnuts, and bamboo can all be polished with sandpaper, sprayed with shellac or clear acrylic, strung on a leather thong, and turned into a necklace or a belt.

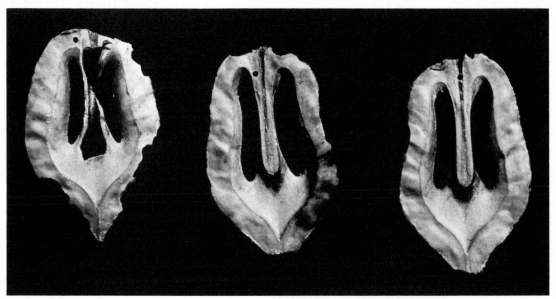

CHRISTMAS WREATHS

A spectacular Christmas wreath might combine lotus pods from your fall vacation in South Carolina with pepper wheat from the central Texas hill country, buckeyes (horse chestnuts) from the Smokies, larch cones from the Northwest, and with spruce cones from the coast of Maine — or any combination of materials from the places you have visited.

Although Hazel Whittington of Mill River Valley, North Carolina, is kept busy on her farm and doesn't travel much, she has made many a vicarious trip thanks to her friends who do travel and come back with souvenirs for her to weave into a friendship wreath.

"It's nice the way they think of me when they go places," she says. "They go off to Florida, California, Arizona — and they don't just tell me afterward what it looked like. They bring back nuts and cones and pods to show me."

Cones, pods, seeds, bracts — the makings of a Christmas wreath.

Kentucky mountain cones and nuts are the ingredients of this Christmas wreath hanging on a New England door. (Mark Lennihan)

Friendship wreath   As soon as she is ready to use these souvenirs, Mrs. Whittington washes them to remove the sand and dries them in the oven. Then she drills a 5/52-inch or a 1/16-inch hole in the nuts or other hard items so that each one may be wired separately to a Masonite frame. Here are her directions:

Materials and Tools

one roll of 20-gauge wire
jack pine, white pine, loblolly, spruce, hemlock, short-leaf pine, balsam cones, and cones from shrubs
masonite pegboard cut into a doughnut shape — or whatever size you wish your wreath to be. When you cut your board, try to arrange it so the first holes are no closer than 1/2 inch from the edge of the board.
buckeyes, hickory nuts, acorns, cotton bolls, hazelnuts, peach seeds, pecans, sweet gum balls, walnuts, cut sections of cones for flowers (try to have a variety of shades of brown and a variety of textures: buckeyes add a rich brown; hickory nuts are blond)
clear plastic acrylic spray
felt
Elmer's glue

1. Snip off 6 to 8 inches of the 20-gauge wire to wire the individual cones that will be attached to the Masonite circle.

Left: Masonite pegboard is the base of the wreath that Hazel Whittington makes of wild things gathered in North Carolina. Right: Rear view of Hazel Whittington's wreath. Felt conceals the masonite on the back.

2. Insert the wire behind the scales of the cones that will be a part of your wreath, two or three scales up from the base of the cone, in a place where the wire slips in easily.

3. Pull one end of the wire out and wind it tightly around the longer twist of wire two or three times to fasten the cone into the Masonite circle.

4. Drill nuts and pits so that they have a 5/52- or 1/16-inch hole across their bases. Drill with care about 1/4 inch up the nut. (Remember that nuts are slippery.) Although you must use a drill to make holes in nuts, an ice pick or awl might be satisfactory for making the holes in pods, Mrs. Whittington points out. If you use acorns, remove the cup before drilling. Insert wire into the holes in the nuts and twist the short wire end to the long with needlenose pliers.

5. For the outside of her wreaths, Mrs. Whittington uses long-leaf pine cones which she sometimes cuts in half with a backsaw or hand band saw. She likes them because they are strong, but you can use almost any cones.

6. Begin at the outside of your wreath. Fit your first cone onto the Masonite edge, pushing the Masonite in between some of the cone scales.

7. Take the wire that is attached to the cone and insert it through one of the holes in the Masonite. Poke the wire up through an adjoining hole and bring it up to the top of the Masonite again, winding it around the cone once more. Go down through a second hole with the wire.

8. Attach a second cone, pushing its scales up into the scales of the first cone. Wire it securely to the Masonite and connect the wires of the first cone with those of the second for greater security. Fill the entire outside edge with cones.

9. Repeat the procedure for the inside rim, but using smaller cones — short-leaf pine cones with the tops cut out, perhaps.

10. Fill in the rest of the space with more cones, some inverted, and with cone flowers, seed pods and nuts. To make an attractive wreath, you should have three points of interest on it. Mrs. Whittington establishes these by having three large cones or cone flowers as the points of interest and filling in with smaller cones and nuts around them.

11. Spray the finished wreath with clear plastic acrylic to preserve the cones and to bring out the textures.

12. Cover the network of wires on the back by gluing a doughnut of felt over them with Elmer's glue.

Note the points of interest that are established to make this wreath a pretty one.

Dorothy Senn's wreath This simpler version of a holiday wreath is made by Dorothy Senn of Oak Ridge, Tennessee.

1. Drill holes through the shells of the nuts you wish to use, employing a hand drill with a 1/16-inch bit and drilling into the nut about 1/2 inch.
2. Wire the cones under the scales and attach florist's wire or toothpicks to the wires.

Left: Cardboard bound with masking tape helps to hang Dorothy Senn's Styrofoam wreath. Right: Florist's picks or toothpicks provide an easy way to attach the nuts and cones when Styrofoam is used as the backing.

3. Buy a Styrofoam ring for the base.
4. From pieces of cardboard, cut four arcs about 3 inches long. Bind them about 2 inches apart around the top of the wreath with brown masking tape. These are reinforcements from which you will hang your wreath.
5. Use an ice pick or awl to make a hole through the masking tape, cardboard, and Styrofoam. Insert heavy florist's wire through the holes, looping the wire together in back.
6. Spray-paint the wreath base floral brown. (Lee Ward's works well. Do not use ordinary spray paint, for it will melt the Styrofoam.)
7. Use the center of the bottom of the wreath as the focal point. One at a time, dip one end of each toothpick in Elmer's glue and then into a pod or nut. (A lotus pod makes a good focal point.) Let it dry. Then dip the other end into the glue and insert it into the Styrofoam at an angle. Try to make a pattern of lights and darks, small items and large. Spray with clear acrylic.

Sweet gum balls are the main attraction in this wreath designed by Eileen Argenziano.

KISSING BALL

Materials

hickory nuts, sweet gum balls, acorns, buckeyes, cloves, hemlock cones
a Styrofoam ball 3 inches in diameter
coat hanger
brown floral spray
clear acrylic spray
gold cord, about 2 feet long
Elmer's glue
ribbon
florist's wire
toothpicks

1. Stick a few cloves and sweet gum balls into which you have glued toothpicks into the Styrofoam ball, which has been presprayed with brown floral spray.
2. Fill in all the spaces with other nuts, as done in Dorothy Senn's wreath, above.
3. With wire clippers, cut a straightened coat hanger into a 5- or 6-inch piece, and use it to poke a hole through the center of the Styrofoam ball. Remove the hanger.
4. Spray-paint the finished ball with clear acrylic spray to give a sheen to the nuts.
5. Thread a double piece of gold cord through the hole that you poked. Make a knot at both the top and bottom of the ball and glue each of them to the ball with Elmer's. Now you have a hanging loop at the top.
6. Make a bow of florist's ribbon. Wrap the center with florist's wire, and at the other end of the wire put a floral pick or toothpick and glue it into the Styrofoam ball at the top.

Sweet gum balls mounted on Styrofoam and sprayed with gold paint make charming kissing balls.

Below: Gold string, gold spray paint, a few seed pearls, and a sweet gum ball glitter on a Christmas tree.

A TOPIARY TREE

Materials

a Styrofoam ball 6 inches in diameter (or smaller if you prefer)
brown floral spray
one 3/4-inch thick dowel of white birch, cut to the length you like
nuts
toothpicks
Elmer's glue
octagon-shaped base for the tree, of birch or any wood that will match
Minwax or clear acrylic lacquer
ribbon

1. Spray the Styrofoam ball with brown floral spray and let it dry.
2. Drill 1 1/2 inches into the ball with a bit large enough to accommodate the dowel.
3. Insert the dowel into the tree, keeping the tree upright while you work.
4. Insert the predrilled nuts on toothpicks, prepared with glue as they were for Mrs. Senn's wreath and the kissing ball, above.
5. Drill a hole in the base and insert the dowel. Varnish the base and dowel or not, as you choose, or stain them with Minwax or spray them with clear acrylic lacquer. Spray the nuts with clear acrylic for sheen.
6. Brighten the tree by attaching a pretty ribbon to the dowel.

Nuts from the woods, a dowel and dowel stand, ribbon, a Styrofoam ball, and toothpicks make an attractive topiary tree.

51

A FOREST CENTERPIECE

Materials

a rectangular piece of cardboard 8 x 16 inches (The size you choose will depend to some extent on the size of your table.)

two rectangular pieces of Styrofoam, one about 2 inches smaller than the other in both the width and length

Sobo glue or linoleum paste

metal candleholders from hobby shops

a variety of cones, acorns, thistles, cotton boll pods, sequoia scales, sweet gum balls

gold acrylic spray paint or spray gloss

1. Glue the two Styrofoam layers together; glue the bottom layer to the heavy cardboard.
2. Glue the candleholders in place on the top layer.
3. Begin with the sequoia scales. Glue them all around the bottom outside edge, curved side up, so that they seem to form little cups for the next layer, which will be small items like sweet gum balls and nuts. Work from the bottom up, and be sure each level is dry before you move on to the next one. Work in small areas.
4. Spray with clear acrylic or gold, silver, or white.

Woodland collectibles from New York State are the ingredients of Eileen Argenziano's centerpiece.

Left: Milkweed pods and teasels lend themselves to Christmas decorations.
Right: Teasels from an autumn walk make many amusing oddments.

Left: Dried flowers brighten milkweed pods.
Right: This country arrangement of moss, sumac berries, cones, and an abandoned wasps' nest was made as a forest remembrance.

Dried grasses, wild grape tendrils, galls, carded sheep wool, and cowhitch vine are part of this Tennessee stitchery by Margaret Young.

Clipped cones and a corn shuck flower are a never-fading bouquet.

54

3

From the surface of the earth
Sand and clay

In most parts of the nation, the traveler who quits the highway and explores side roads will profit more from his vacation than the driver who speeds along the Interstates from one metropolis to another. Passing through little towns and villages may lengthen your travel time, but towns and villages comprise America — white clapboard in New England, gray fieldstone in New Jersey and Pennsylvania, red brick in the Midwest and the South, red adobe in the Southwest. A beach is the obvious place to find sand, but inland, off the main routes, roads cut into hills, and this is where much of the country's colored sand and clay can be found.

Souvenir shops sell colored sand in bottles and clay ashtrays and vases to remind the visitor of the Smokies or the Ozarks or the Natchez Trace. Sand paintings — though not the genuine ones done outdoors by Navajo and Apache medicine men for tribal ceremonies — are available, too, at gift shops. But there is no need to buy such souvenirs. With a little patience, you can fill your own bottles with colored sand and mold the gay clay you find into artifacts. Before collecting sand and clay, however, make sure the law allows you to pick them up. Colored sand may not be taken from the Painted Desert of Arizona, and the clay from Martha's Vineyard's Gay Head Cliffs is similarly protected. But there are many parts of the country where sand and clay are simply turned up and left by the roadside when a new road is built.

SAND IN BOTTLES

Doyle Blalock of Little Rock, Mississippi, is a rural postman and a sand-in-bottles artist who knows of many such roads winding through east-central Mississippi, and he advises the traveler in the South seeking colorful sand simply to inquire in the various states as to where this or that county digs the sand for its roads. The most colorful sands in the Southeast, Mr. Blalock says, are in the chain of hills that run from Memphis, Tennessee, through Mobile, Alabama, to Meridian, Mississippi. He adds, "Anywhere in the South where you see hills of red clay, you will probably also find red and purple and pink sand. We have yellow sand, too — from a deep gold color to a light, light yellow. About the only color we don't have in Mississippi is blue. There's one kind that looks blue when it's wet, but when you take it home and dry it out, it turns purple." Drying, he goes on to say, is a most important part of working with sand.

Here are his directions for preparing sand bottles:

Materials

old newspaper
colored sands of various hues
a funnel
a teaspoon
a clear glass bottle (for beginners, a miniature Welch grape juice bottle is good)
a straightened coat hanger or a lead pencil
a dowel or cut-off broom handle
paraffin

1. Place five layers of newspaper in your yard and spread out the sand you have collected to dry on it (different colors in different piles, of course).
2. Every 30 minutes or so, turn the sand to speed the drying process. On a sunny day, most sand should be dry in 3 or 4 hours. But be sure before using it that it is thoroughly dry or it will not fall into your bottle properly.
3. There will almost always be lumps of clay in brightly colored sand, so when the sand is dry, use a rolling pin to crush them.
4. Sift out any lumps that remain.
5. Using the funnel and teaspoon, put about 1/2 inch of one color into your bottle. Then add 1/2 inch or so of another color.
6. Poke your hanger or the point of a pencil into the top layer of sand near the outside of the bottle. Poke all the way down into the bottom layer. By so doing, of course, you will be pushing the top sand color into the bottom color. Choose a pattern you would like to make and work at creating it — waves or a zigzag, for instance — and go all the way around the bottle with it.
7. Repeat steps 5 and 6, varying the patterns and the shades of sand you

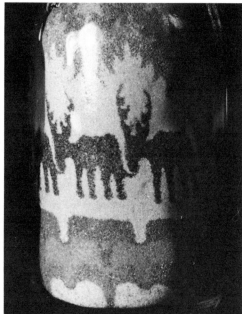

Left: Colored clay can be layered like parfait into glass containers. Animals as well as geometric designs can be made from colored sand in bottles once you acquire the knack of it. With the aid of a coat hanger, Doyle Blalock drew these reindeer in colored sand from the Mississippi hills. (Alison Shaw)

use, until you reach the point where the bottle begins to curve toward the mouth.

8. Stop adding sand and use the coat hanger or pencil to pack the sand tight. To do this, thrust the wire into the center of the sand and work it up and down several times so the sand falls. You may find that you will need to add another layer of sand. Keep adding sand and poking until the sand is within 1/8 inch from the top.

9. When there is no longer any give to the sand, poke a dowel or a broom handle into the mouth of the bottle. Stack magazines or newspapers on a table to act as a cushion. Holding the dowel or broom handle in the bottle top, bump the bottle on the cushion of magazines several times to pack the sand still harder. Unless it is truly packed hard, Mr. Blalock says, it will not stay in layers or in a design. If you need to add more sand during this process, do so.

10. When you are sure the sand is pressed as hard as possible and the bottle is filled to 1/8 inch from the rim, fold up a small piece of paper towel and put it on top of the sand. Drop a little melted paraffin on top of this as a seal and cap the bottle.

When you have perfected your bottle-filling technique, try working with large bottles — whiskey bottles, decanters, and the like. You might wish to use one of them as the base for a lamp.

SAND PAINTING

Although sand painting can be very complex, this method is simple enough to do with children. Wenonah Silva of Gay Head, Massachusetts, is a Wampanoag Indian who has studied the sand-painting techniques of her southwestern Indian brothers. Although their sand paintings were never meant to stay — they were drawn on the ground after sunset, to be finished and destroyed by sunrise, or at sunrise, to be finished and destroyed by sunset — Mrs. Silva's paintings are permanent. Sometimes she uses a driftwood base for them. At other times, when she is teaching Indian children about sand painting, she uses a sandpaper base for simplicity's sake. To make a sand painting as she does, follow these directions:

Materials

plywood and sandpaper or flat driftwood and beige sand
Elmer's glue
colored sands, pulverized coal, powdered roots, bark, or seeds
Hypla Hygel (available in crafts stores)
Damar varnish (available in crafts stores)

1. If you use driftwood, first you must seal it. Give the driftwood a light coating with a solution of equal parts of Elmer's glue and water. Do this three times, letting the glue dry between the first two applications. After the third application, sprinkle beige sand on it as your base. Let it dry. If you use plywood, apply the glue to the plywood and then glue on the sandpaper. Place a weight on it and let it dry. (If you don't do this, the painting will buckle.)

2. If there is no black sand available where you are but there are coal deposits, use coal as a substitute by wrapping it in a cloth and rolling or hammering it until the particles are small enough to go through a sieve.

3. Spray the sand and coal you plan to use with Damar varnish, and spread it out on a newspaper to dry. The varnish both brightens the colors in the sand and keeps it from flying everywhere as you are trying to incorporate it into your painting.

4. Sketch a design for your painting on a piece of paper and either lightly resketch it on the sand (using dressmaker's carbon; it is the only material with which you can draw on sandpaper, Mrs. Silva says) or put it beside your work so you can copy it readily. Begin with a simple design.

5. Start with the darkest colors you wish to use. Apply a light coat of Elmer's to the area where you want the dark color. Sift the sand onto

58

the area. Leave it on the painting to dry for about an hour. Then shake off any excess.

6. Sift the next darkest color you are using onto the areas designated for that color. Let them dry. Shake off the excess. Apply the lightest colors last.

7. Let the painting "rest" for 72 hours. Then vacuum it with the brush attachment on your vacuum cleaner.

8. Spray the painting lightly with Damar.

9. If, after you have completed one section of the painting, you are displeased with it and wish dark hair to be darker or fuller, for instance, you can always apply second and third layers of sand until you achieve the richness that you wish.

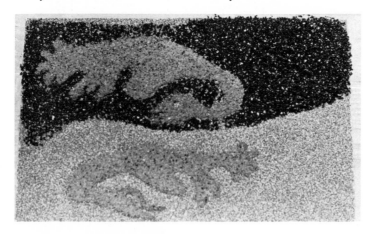

Above: These dragons in the sand were made by a Gay Head Indian child.

Left: A southwestern Indian sand painting. (Robert McCrystal)

59

A contemporary Indian sand painting. (Mark Lennihan)

Left: For an Indian sand painting done a modern way, these ingredients are necessary. Right: Wampanoag Indian Wenonah Silva applies Elmer's glue to sandpaper to start an indoor sand painting.

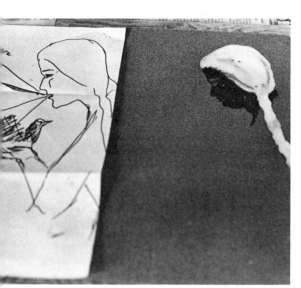

Left: The sand-painting artist sketches a design on paper before work begins in the sand. Right: Sifting is an important step in sand painting today's way.

SAND SCULPTURE

The simplest of all sand crafts, of course — and ideal for a beachfront holiday — is making plaster casts of fish, starfish, and shells to hang on the wall.

To sand-cast on the beach, scoop a rectangular hollow in the wet sand with a shingle. Press a starfish or scallop shell or a combination of starfish and shells, and perhaps even a small fish you have caught and frozen to make it stiff, into the sand. Remove the shells and fish and gently spoon in plaster of paris, mixed according to the directions on the package. Stir it slowly while mixing it so no bubbles form. It is ready to use when it is about the consistency of light cream. Work carefully but fast, for plaster of paris hardens quickly.

When the plaster is slightly set, lay a square of screen cut to fit exactly over the back of the piece into it and press it into place. Eventually you will tie a loop of wire through this screening in order to hang the plaque. Plaster of paris is heavy, and the screen is necessary to provide support for the hanging.

Variations of this technique include imbedding decorative shells and beach glass in the plaster of paris by leaving them in the sand hollow while you pour in the plaster of paris, rather than removing them before starting your pouring. Artist-photographer Clare Barnes laid a picture frame in the sand, arranged shells and stones inside it, and poured plaster of paris over it for an especially attractive beach memento.

If you wait until you are home from vacation to do your casting, you can put several inches of sand in the bottom of a Sara Lee coffee cake pan, do your imprinting, let the cast harden, and remove it simply by cutting the pan away.

SAND-CAST CANDLES

Candles can be made in the damp sand at the beach but are easier to do in a pail at home. Dig an indentation of the size and shape you would like your candle to be in the damp sand. (For example, for a starfish-shaped candle, press a starfish into the sand.) Melt paraffin over hot water. To color the candle, try adding a quart of clover leaves to the hot wax. The color you will get is very light, so even for one candle you will need a great many leaves. You will have to strain them out after they have added their color, but it is worth the trouble. If you prefer, you can use crayon chips to color the wax.

This seashore sand casting is the beachcombing work of Virginia Smith. (George McAllister)

The frame became an integral part of this Clare Barnes sand casting. (George Adams)

Remove the starfish — or whatever you have used to make your shape — from the sand. Tie a washer to the end of a wick or a piece of string that will serve as your wick. Place it in the indentation. Tie the other end of the wick to a dowel and place it across your sand pit or pail.

Pour the hot wax into the indentation. The hotter the wax, the more sand you will have on the outside of your candle when you are through. Leave the wax in the hole to harden for a day. The next day, there will probably be a slight indentation in the center of your candle. Poke it with an ice pick or awl and pour in a little more wax. Let the candle set for 48 hours. It should then be cured, and you should have a sand-dusted candle.

WINDJAMMERS

When wintry winds whistle under the door of your year-round home, you can keep them out with a draft stopper, or windjammer, filled with sand from the beach near your summer home. To make one, cut a rectangle of cotton long enough to cover the window or door crack and 8 to 10 inches wide. If you have leftover curtain or upholstery material it would be especially attractive, for it would then match your drapes or upholstery. If you are artistic, of course, you can use plain, unbleached cotton and draw your own designs on it.

Stitch the material up like a pillow, leaving one end open so you can pour in the sand. Be sure to use sand that comes from high on the beach, for if it is close to the tide line it will contain salt, and it will never dry out. Turn the case inside out and fill it — but not too full, for it must have flexibility if it is to fit into the nooks and crannies of most door and window cracks. Sew it closed.

A windjammer like this one will keep the drafts out of your home. (Thomas D. Stevens)

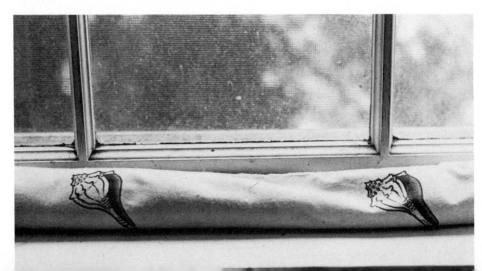

Beach sand fills the casing that makes this pretty bookend by Virginia Smith. (Mark Lennihan)

CLAY POTTERY

Although clay must be fired in a kiln for strength, colored clay loses all of its natural color when fired. Since much of the clay one finds by the roadside and on beaches is a mellow brick red or gray, the vacationer will probably prefer to forgo hardness in favor of preserving the natural color.

To make simple items of sun-baked clay, collect the clay as free from sand as possible. If the clay is dry, you will have to moisten it before you can work it. Put a large chunk of it into a 1-pound coffee can and cover it with water. Let it soak until it is the consistency of cream. Run your fingers through it and remove any stones and large particles of sand. You can pour it through a sieve, but that is usually not necessary. Work indoors, and fast, for clay hardens quickly. When you have removed all of the stones, start modeling.

The clay for this pottery was dug from Tennessee roadcuts by Harold Lane of the Pigeon Forge Pottery.

Harold Lane's turtle is of rolled and pinched pottery.

Pinch pot This is a good, simple pot to make. Roll a ball in your hands and make an indentation in it to be the mouth of the pot or vase. Put the pot on newspapers in the sun to dry. When it is thoroughly dry, spray-shellac it. This will both bring out the colors and make your pot more durable than most sun-dried pots, according to Ronnie Simon of Gay Head, Massachusetts, a pottery teacher.

Coil pot You can fashion a coil pot of varied shades of clay, using snakes of gray, red, yellow, and white. Form the coils into a vase form; smooth the snakes together and sun-bake. Again, shellac to bring out the color.

"Molded" pot Roll clay dough to about a 3/8-inch thickness and drape it over a rock with a shape you like. Leave it in the sun until it is partly, but not entirely, hard — "leather hard" is the potter's term. Lift it off the rock carefully and let it dry fully right side up.

Unbaked pottery keeps its
natural colors, though it is much
less sturdy than fired pottery.

These clay beads were designed
and molded by Marion
Monaghan of McLean, Virginia.

CLAY BEADS

These will have to be fired. Roll a coil of clay about 1 inch in diameter. Cut it up into pieces the size you wish your beads to be. Make a hole through each bead with a nail. There may be a certain amount of shrinkage, so don't use too small a nail. Decorate the beads however you choose, making designs with a nail. If you plan to use stones, press them into the beads before firing, then remove them when the beads go to the kiln. When the beads return, glue the stones into their setting with 5-minute epoxy.

Even if you have no kiln of your own, firing your beads should cost less than a cent a bead. Ask to have them fired in a low fire. When they are done, string them on a leather thong or waxed linen. For a more decorative string of beads, make macramé knots between them. At most small potteries you can ask to have your work fired.

You can decorate the clay you find with the imprint of a dried leaf or Queen Anne's lace and make it into a pendant. To do this:

1. Let your clay dry out a little. Then pat it into the shape you wish your pendant to be, but make it slightly thicker than you want for the final product, for there will be shrinkage.
2. With a large malted milk straw or the blunt end of a pencil, poke a hole through the top of the pendant so you can string it.
3. Press the back of a leaf onto the pendant. Poplar, oak, and fern leaves imprint well. If you want to imprint a flower, be sure it isn't a limp one. Bluets do nicely. You can even imprint a pine seedling.
4. With tweezers, remove the leaf or flower from the clay. Let the pendant dry.
5. Brush the clay piece with Barnard or Albany slip, available at any pottery supplies shop. Barnard slip will give a flat finish; Albany, a shiny one. Follow the package directions.
6. With a sponge, wipe off all the excess slip. This will make your design stand out, for the slip will remain only in the indentation.
7. Take your piece to a local ceramics shop to have it baked. Ask to have it fired at Cone 6.
8. String your finished earth-colored piece onto a leather thong.

Shells and wildflowers can be put into clay pendants.

The back of a leaf rather than the front should be pressed into clay for a pendant.

Delicate wildflowers and grasses can be imprinted in clay to make napkin rings.

4
Shell and fish crafts

Wherever there are bodies of water, there are shells in lesser or greater variety — delicate transparent toenail shells, chalky clamshells, smooth chestnut-brown cowries, iridescent abalones, graceful scallops, channeled whelks. The vacationing beachgoer is sure to find them, particularly if he strolls the sand after a storm.

Long ago, the North American Indians recognized shells' beauty and their value; they called them "wampum" and used them as jewelry and money. Today's vacationer, like the Indian, often recognizes their beauty and collects them, decorating a bookshelf or a corner curio cabinet with them. But much more than that can be done.

An egg carton makes an ideal collecting box for young beachcombers.

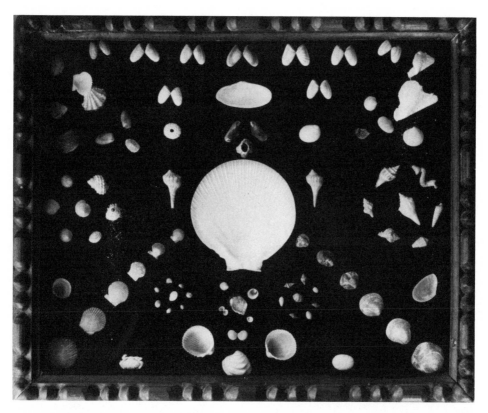

This tray of shells under glass was arranged by New Englander Jane Farrow after a Florida trip. (Peter Simon)

Wild roses sit prettily in a Cape Cod shell vase.

Mementos of a shelling holiday in Florida can be set under glass to make a decorative coffee table or a pretty bathroom mirror.

Shells can embellish Styrofoam ice buckets, transform old fashioned glasses into candleholders, make a hanging shell lamp for a beach house, or make the finishing touch on kitchen canisters for a summer house.

Bookends can be brightened with shells; so can cocktail toothpicks, notepaper, and jewelry boxes. Of course, shells also make pretty jewelry, figurines, flowers that never wilt, and Christmas decorations.

To prepare shells for such uses, Virginia Smith of Oak Bluffs, Massachusetts, who spends long waterfront winters at shellcraft, advises cleaning them with care.

PREPARING SHELLS

Cleaning

1. Wash your shells in warm, soapy water. If necessary, soak them in a solution of 1/4 cup Clorox in a little less than 1 quart of water for a while to remove any foreign matter.
2. Wipe the shells dry gently. If you are using shells that are not white, apply a little lemon oil or a similar oil (that will not turn rancid) to the top surface of the shell with a soft cloth, but be sure that the surface that you plan to glue is not oiled or the glue will not stick.

Gluing To strengthen the shells you plan to attach to a surface, saturate a piece of absorbent cotton that will fit inside your shell with Duco cement or epoxy, and place it in the shell cavity. (To properly saturate the ball of cotton, you may need to poke it around in the cement with a toothpick.) The cotton you use should be large enough to touch most of the entire inside surface of the shell, but it should not be so large that it can be seen when pressed into place. If you use epoxy, which is especially good for gluing to metal, work quickly, for it dries very fast.

Sea scallop, bay scallop, toenail, and whelk shells all readily become part of the shellcrafter's art. (Alison Shaw)

BOOKENDS

One of the simplest ways Mrs. Smith has of using the shells she gathers is on bookends.

1. Buy plain, 5-inch-tall teak bookends from an office supply or crafts store or by mail order. (The Sunset House catalogue offers them.)
2. Cut a piece of 1/4-inch twisted rope or cord to the exact measurement of the outside edges and top of each bookend. Taper both ends of each rope and pinch them flat with a little glue to keep them from unraveling before they are attached.
3. Glue the rope around the top and sides of each bookend and hold it in place with a succession of rubber bands until it is dry.
4. Select a variety of shells to enhance the ends of the bookends. Stuff the shells you choose with glue-soaked cotton cut to fit.
5. Glue the shells into whatever arrangement you wish. A spray of fan coral or a tiny piece of driftwood glued on with the shells can be an attractive addition.

Teak bookends take on a new character when decorated with souvenir shells.

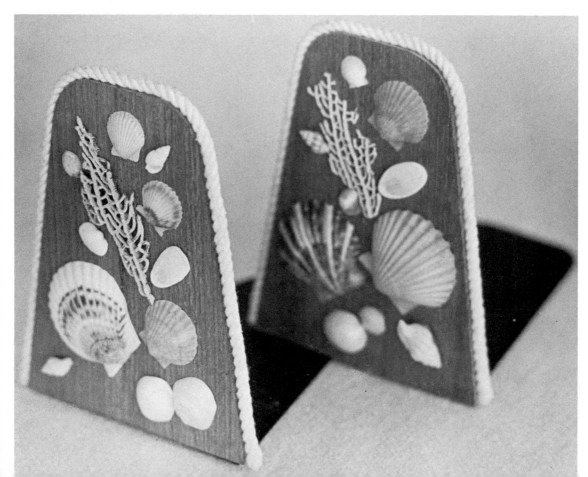

Tiny slipper or boat shells, painted with airplane model paint to resemble beetles or mushrooms or flowers, can be attractively glued to the top of notepaper. Fill the shells with a tiny dot of glue-soaked cotton, following the instructions above. Then lay them on a piece of newspaper or typing paper while you decorate them so that the cotton attaches itself to the paper. When the paint is dry, cut the shells from the paper and apply a little glue to the bottom of the paper on which they have dried. This will give them a smooth base. Arrange them attractively at the top of your notepaper. If you like, you can make additional decorations, such as sea gulls, stems, or leaves, with Magic Markers around the shells on the notepaper.

BASKET BAG WITH SHELLS

1. Buy an inexpensive flat basket bag at a roadside basket market, or use a bag with basket sides and a wooden top.
2. If you use a flat basket bag, lay it on its side and spread the shells you wish displayed in a pleasing arrangement.
3. One by one, remove the shells and insert a glue-saturated cotton wad inside them (see instructions for preparing shells, above). The wad, in this case, need not fill the entire shell, but it should be large enough to form a firm gluing surface to join the shell with the basket. Be sure the glue does not ooze out the sides of the shells as you attach them.

Tiny slipper or boat shells decorate summer notepaper.

74

4. Let the shells dry before you turn the basket upright. Since some shells crack easily, don't decorate the side of the bag that will be next to your body.

5. Follow the same general procedure if you are decorating a bag with a flat top. If the top is varnished, you may have to scratch the varnish so the glue will stick. Either of these bags may be made more attractive by sewing in a gay lining and tacking it to the basket corners.

Remember your beach vacation with a shell-topped pocketbook like this one, designed by Miriam Richardson.

Perfect for a sunny day at the beach or in the garden is this gay shell hat.

A Shell Bracelet

1. Buy a bracelet backing at a crafts or jewelry supply store.
2. Use shells that are just about the same size as the backing.
3. Fill the shells with epoxy-saturated cotton (see instructions for preparing shells, above).
4. Glue them in place on the backing.

A Scallop Shell Neck Circlet

1. Select a plain silver- or gold-colored neck circlet at a crafts supply shop.
2. If you plan to attach three scallop shells, buy six 1/4-inch jump rings at the same shop to match the circlet. (You will need two rings for each shell.)
3. Lay your shell carefully against a small block of wood for support and carefully drill two holes in each shell wing — one at each end — with an electric drill and a No. 60 to 65 drill bit. A safer method is to patiently scratch back and forth with the tip of a scribe or gimlet until you have your holes. (Experiment a little with shells that are not your favorites so that you get the knack of making the holes, for scallop shells are delicate and break easily.)
4. Open the jump rings and slip them into the holes you have drilled. Then close the rings and slip them onto the circlet.

An Ocean-Tumbled Necklace

Kate Taylor likes to walk the beaches of Gay Head, Massachusetts, looking for ocean-tumbled bits of purple quahog (clam) shell. When she has found enough to make a necklace, she lines them up according to size and color in two lines — the smallest shell bits at the top; the biggest, heaviest ones at the bottom.

With a 1/16-inch bit in a hand drill, and applying a minimum amount of pressure against a breadboard, she drills a hole in each piece of shell. With her hand drill, she uses a stream of water from a baby bottle to keep the drill cool during this process. Also, she says that it's a good idea when drilling small shell bits to take a candle and drip a little wall of wax onto the board. Then you can hold your shell in place against the wax while you are drilling.

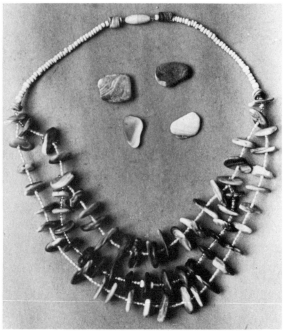

Left: A scallop shell circlet at the neck of a sweater brings a touch of summer to winter. Right: Ocean-tumbled clamshells and beads were made into this necklace by Kate Taylor.

When she has drilled enough shells for a necklace — of one, two, or three strands, depending on the number of shells — she strings them onto 10- to 15-pound monofilament fish line with glass beads or seed pearls in between.

Tumbled bits of quahog shell with two holes drilled in them also make handsome buttons.

Either a hand drill or a power drill can be used to make holes in shells, but always drill with care and expect to break some shells.

Left: Scallop shells — orange, pink, golden, pure white — with a touch of greenery become a holiday corsage. Right: Scallop shells should be wired around the wings and stuffed with cotton before they are glued onto hard surfaces. (Alison Shaw)

A Scallop Corsage

1. Shells for a corsage should be about 1 inch in diameter and in assorted colors (some scallop shells are pinkish on the surface; others are orange, golden, or pure white). Prepare nine or ten shells by washing them in Clorox and wiping them with lemon oil.
2. One wing of each shell has a natural notch. With a nail file or emery board, make a matching notch on the opposite wing.
3. Fold an 8-inch strand of 28-gauge household wire in half and slide the fold into one of the wing notches and pinch it in place.
4. With the rounded side of the shell facing you, stretch the top strand of the folded wire down to the point of the shell and bend it under the opposite wing of the shell, sliding it into the notch in that wing. Bring it back down to the point of the shell, and, under the point, twist it together with the understrand of folded wire to make a stem. Wrap this stem with floral tape, starting at the base of the shell. Repeat this procedure with each shell.
5. Form a fan by twisting the stems of these individual shells together and bending them into a graceful, curved central stem.
6. Attach a bow to the stem just below the bottom shell.
7. Wire small sprays of greens, real or artificial, behind the corsage, and attach a corsage pin.

Snow white shells and silver Christmas balls are combined by Virginia Smith into a
holiday doorspray.

Holiday Door Spray

Materials

nine to eleven large white scallop shells (do not oil)
six scallop shells of graduated size (do not oil)
one roll 22-gauge household wire
one roll green floral tape
silver spray paint (optional)
24 inches of 11-gauge aluminum wire (from an electrical supply store)
three 1 1/4-inch Christmas balls
one 1 3/4-inch Christmas ball
1 yard red suede Christmas ribbon, 2 to 3 inches wide
four or five sprays of greens, real or artificial

1. Spray paint shells if desired; then wire all of the shells individually as
   for the scallop corsage, but with the 22-gauge wire to support the
   larger shells.
2. Wrap each stem, as before, with green tape.
3. Arrange the nine to eleven shells in a fan shape, with the hollow side
   facing you, and, one at a time, twist the stems together. In making
   your arrangement, be sure that one of the shells is centered at the base
   of the fan.

79

A circle of aluminum wire "cradles" a shell doorspray.

4. Take one of the 1 1/4-inch Christmas balls and, using the household wire, attach it to the stem of the spray, centering it in the center shell.
5. Make a large circle of the aluminum wire to use as a cradle to give back support to the fan of shells. Leave a tail of wire at the bottom of the circle.
6. Take the six graduated scallop shells. Put the two largest matching shells on each side of the wired 1 3/4-inch Christmas ball and twist the three stems together — but not too tightly or the ball will bulge from between the shells. Do the same with the smaller shells and balls.
7. An inch below the base of the fan, wire the largest shells and ball. Three inches below that, wire the second pair, etc. The last unit should be wired 2 inches from the tip of the wire tail.
8. Wrap the entire big stem with floral tape so that it covers all of the wires used to attach the shells.
9. Make six 5-inch loops of the red ribbon in a fan shape to place at the base of the spray. Nest these under the spray in the aluminum support circle, wiring them into place.
10. Wire whatever greenery you wish behind the entire arrangement.

All sorts of Christmas decorations can be made from souvenirs of the summer beach. Miniature horseshoe crabs, starfish, sea horses, sea urchins, smooth sea scallops, ordinary small crab shells — all look elegant brightened with silver or gold spray paint and dangled from a Christmas tree.

Christopher Murphy of Chilmark, Massachusetts, advises, however, that if delicate miniature horseshoe crabs are used, they should be sprayed on both sides with several coats of clear acrylic to give them strength. They can then be gilded as desired.

Dangling Christmas Scenes

Materials

smooth sea scallop shells or ordinary crab shells
spray paint
sequins
Super Duco cement
bayberries, holly, grasses and weeds, straw flowers, jewelry findings,
miniature cones, pine cone scales, miniature ceramic mice, etc., from the
five-and-ten-cent store
plastic fish line (for hanging)

1. Once your shell has been cleaned and dried, spray-paint it. Sprinkle on sequins as you wish and let it dry.
2. Using Duco cement, glue grasses, miniature cones, mice, etc., inside the shell to make a scene.
3. With an electric drill, make a hole at the top of the shell and string the plastic line through it. Again, use no more than a 1/16-inch drill bit.

A Christmas Starfish

The starfish you gather as mementos of beach walks should be laid out flat, with the underside down on a piece of wood, and left outdoors where the rain will wash them and the sun dry them. This will take a week or more. (But if you have several rainy days, bring them inside for they should not stay wet too long or they will rot.)

When the fish are dry, spray-paint them with an undercoat of white. Let them dry and then spray-paint the tips with brass or gold or silver spray paint. With Duco cement, attach a gilded hemlock or tiny pine cone, artificial or real greenery, and the like. Drill a small hole in the end of one tentacle and thread plastic fishing line through it.

Every year, starfish are readied like this for Christmas by Dr. and Mrs. John E. Wallace. (Mark Lennihan)

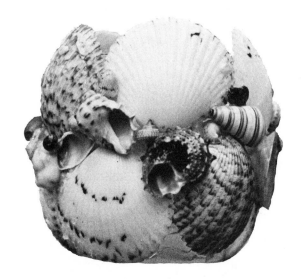

Florida shells are glued to
an old fashioned glass to
become a candleholder.
(Alison Shaw)

SHELL CANDLES

If you are in Florida, follow the advice of Helen Bruns of Deerfield Beach,
and go shell-hunting whenever sand has just been dredged from the
bottom to enlarge an existing beach. Then limpets and cowries and sand
dollars, Scotch bonnets with their upturned "brims," sea scallops and
pink-chambered whelks are everywhere. If the whelks are whole, attach
them at the bottom to a flat shell base; then fill them with melted wax and
a wick and they will make attractive candle centerpieces for a summer
dinner.

Candles and shells may also be combined the way Betty West of
Jensen Beach, Florida, does:

1. Take an 8-ounce old fashioned glass and lay it on its side (resting
   against something, of course, so that it won't roll).
2. Rest two shells on it, as if they were starting a row, top to bottom, on
   the glass. The top shell should extend over the rim of the glass and
   conceal it.
3. Squeeze Elmer's glue all around them so that each shell is resting in a
   glue pool. Let the shells dry in place.
4. With these shells as a wall to keep the next shells from sliding, attach
   two more shells beside them. Let those dry, and continue in this way
   until the glass is covered with shells (all top shells should extend over
   the rim of the glass).

5. Spray the shells with silicone spray to give a shiny effect.
6. Melt enough wax in the center of the glass to stabilize an 8-hour warning candle (it's just the right size to sit, concealed, inside the glass). When you are burning the candle, add a tablespoon of water so the wax that melts will not be so difficult to remove from the glass when you want to insert a fresh candle.

SHELL FLOWERS

The vacation beach can also be remembered year-round if a pot or bouquet of shell flowers sits on the mantelpiece. Each winter, Ruth Nerney shells on Florida's Captiva and Sanibel islands and along Marco Beach. She finds toenail shells that are silver and gray as well as golden, miniature quahog shells, long, thin olive shells, and sea urchins and fashions them into miniature floral arrangements that make table centerpieces when fresh flowers aren't available.

Pansies in miniature

Materials

tiny clam shells
Elmer's glue
florist's wire
plastic top from Spry, Crisco, or coffee can (for a working surface)
Tester's paint

1. For each flower, use five tiny clam shells. Glue two pairs back to back with the sharp hinge points up, the hollowed side out. Let them dry.
2. Glue a single shell, rounded side out and hinge point down, to the center of the cupped pairs.
3. When all of the flower petals are dry, lay a piece of florist's wire with green tape around it on the plastic can top next to the flower. Curl and flatten one end of the wire slightly. Apply a dab of Elmer's glue to the top of the wire.
4. Place the flower on the wire where you have applied the glue. Let it dry where you have laid it.
5. Paint a purple face on the center of the flower with Tester's paints.
6. Four smaller shells of the same variety, glued back to back (there need be no center) and painted lavender, will make forget-me-nots.

Tiny clam shells can
become miniature pansies.

Those striped bass scales all
over the back porch
become miniature roses
when you take a bit of glue
or florist's clay and attach
them to a beach rock.

Miniature roses

Materials

driftwood, shell, shingle, or beach stone (as a base)
Elmer's glue or florist's clay
fish scales (striped bass scales do nicely) or toenail shells. (If you use scales, soak them in cold water a few days; then let them dry in the sun.)

1. Put a glob of Elmer's glue or florist's clay on the driftwood, shell, shingle, or stone. If you use glue, let it set for 20 to 30 minutes until it is gummy and has a slight crust but is not so hard that the shells or scales will not stand up straight in it.
2. Start in the center of the flower with two or three tightly curled "petals" that will look like the inside of a rosebud. Insert the shells by dipping the pointed hinge of each shell into a little more glue than you have affixed to the base, and hold each shell upright in place for 5 to 6 minutes before adding the next shell.
3. Make as many flower clusters as you like. There's no need for stems on these rosebuds, and if you use a variety of shades of toenail shells — grays, golds, silvers — there's no need to paint them, either.

Fish scale forsythia   Lena Knowles and May Harden of Riviera Beach, Florida, are two of a very few Floridians who still know how to turn shells and scales from the shore and sea into full-size flowers — no miniature buds these, but full-scale forsythia and pussy willows for springtime bouquets. Mrs. Harden's directions for fish scale forsythia are:

1. Catch two fish, preferably giant sea bass or jewfish, and scale them.
2. Soak the scales in cold water for several days — outdoors and covered, for the scales smell.
3. Wash any remaining meat off and let the scales dry in the shade (never in the sun or the scales will curl).
4. Dye the scales yellow in warm dye.
5. With a needle, an ice pick, or an awl, punch a small hole in each scale and wire four petals together (through the holes) using tin-coated copper wire, No. 24, 28, or 30. Repeat until all the scales are used.
6. Take stamens you have purchased in a crafts store. Center one in each flower. Wrap the wires at the base of the scales, with the stamens inside, tightly with embroidery floss. Tie with a buttonhole stitch.

It's spring year round if you make a forsythia of giant sea bass scales and a pussy willow of Florida cowrie shells. (Alison Shaw)

7. Attach twenty-seven of the flowers to a No. 16 or 18 galvanized wire. There should be one at the top, then pairs extending the length of the stem.
8. Wrap the wire stem in green-dyed raffia held in place with a little Elmer's glue at the end.

Cowrie shell pussy willows

1. With a darning needle, punch a hole in the base of fifteen cowrie shells.
2. With tin-coated copper wire, No. 24, 28, or 30, attach them to a No. 16 or 18 galvanized wire stem in the pattern of pussy willows.
3. Wrap the stem in brown-dyed raffia, glued at the bottom with Elmer's glue.

An olive shell stem and a sea urchin cap make this souvenir toadstool. (Alison Shaw)

Sea urchin toadstools

Materials

large shelf of tree fungus or a piece of driftwood
olive shells
Elmer's glue
firm, dry sea urchins
greenery, dried flowers, etc.

1. Drill holes large enough to accommodate the pointed ends of the olive shells in the driftwood (or ream the holes with a penknife if you use fungus).
2. Dip the ends of the olive shells in the glue and let them dry. Then put more glue on top of the cotton. Reverse each sea urchin, fitting each over one of the olive shells set in the fungus or driftwood. The olive shells make the stems of the toadstools. You will have to hold the urchins in place for a while to let them dry.
3. Glue artificial greenery, Florida holly, British soldiers, lichens — as you like — in your arrangement.

A vase fashioned from turkey shells and a sea urchin is filled with miniature shell flowers.

Shell flowers in an urchin vase

1. For the feet of your sea urchin vase, lay two miniature turkey wing shells on a piece of wax paper, open side down. With Elmer's glue, attach a sea urchin, open side up, to the turkey wings. Put florist's clay in the sea urchin cup and arrange beach grass, pearly everlasting, or these tiny shell flowers in it.
2. If you find a sea urchin that is not thoroughly dry, you can use the pretty little "flowerette" in the center in your bouquet. Soak the urchin in a mixture of 1/3 Clorox and 2/3 water for a few minutes. Then remove the spines and the insides with a penknife, taking care not to cut the "flowerette" at the top of the inside. Separate it from the rest and glue it, flowerette side up, to a bit of florist's wire wrapped in tape and put it in your urchin vase.
3. Two cochina shells just as they come out of the sand, still joined, make a pretty bud. Gently twist taped florist's wire around the hinge to make the stem. Remember that little shells are very fragile.

Children always enjoy Ruth Nerney's shell pictures. With acrylics, oils, or water colors, paint a face on the bottom two-thirds of a quahog shell set the long way. Paint the top third to look like the peak of a sou'wester hat.

When the paint is dry, press glue-saturated cotton into the shell. Put more glue on the outside rim of the shell and glue it to a piece of cardboard or a shingle.

When it has dried in place, paint the rest of the slicker hat and a slicker on the background.

Point side up, a quahog shell makes a fine coolie hat or a sunbonnet. A mussel shell makes a bonnet for Miss Minnie Mussel. All of these pictures, framed, decorate a children's room attractively.

A sunbonnet or a coolie hat? Either way, it had its beginnings in a quahog shell.

A quahog shell makes the face and hat for a picture of an old-time fisherman.

SAND DOLLAR JEWELRY

When strollers on Florida's Sanibel Island go out waist deep at low tide, they can gather sand dollars while they are still alive and use them as pendants or on earrings the way Rhode Island vacationer Clinton H. Cram does. "Don't wait to pick them up on the beach," he advises. "They'll be too dry and fragile to use in jewelry."

1. Put the sand dollars in a bath of half Clorox, half water, to whiten them. Then let them dry in the sun about two days, turning them while they dry.
2. Squeeze Elmer's glue, full strength, from the bottle. Dip your finger in water and then in the glue and spread it over the sand dollar on both sides. Let the glue dry and repeat.
3. With Tester's enamel, paint designs around the design in the center of the sand dollar. The sand dollar's markings lend themselves especially well to a poinsettia decoration at Christmastime.
4. Let the paint dry and spray the sand dollar with a triple thick crystal clear glaze available at most craft shops.
5. With Beach Gloo (made by the Beach Co., Ltd., of Fort Myers, Florida) or with Elmer's, glue a jewelry finding to which you can attach a chain to the top of the sand dollar. If the sand dollars are little, you might wish to turn them into earrings instead.
6. If you prefer an undecorated sand dollar, simply spray the dry creature with two coats of Rustoleum, letting each coat dry before the next one is applied. On top of that, spray Speedy Dry gold paint.

When Rhode Islander Clinton H. Cram vacations in Florida, he collects sand dollars in all sizes. He has turned one pair into earrings. (Alison Shaw)

Enamel is the medium that decorates this sand dollar pendant.
(Alison Shaw)

A sand dollar and a decal make
this decorative piece.

91

SHELL DOLLS

Bettyanne Twigg, the author of *The Collector's Guide to Fabric Dolls from 300 B.C. to 1941,* has a pair of shell-dressed 1840 dolls in her collection. Since she is a craftsperson and shell collector as well as a doll collector, she proposes that today's shell collector might like to take a lesson from the past and dress a modern doll in shells.

1. Cut a piece of muslin that will be the right length for the skirt of your doll. (A 6-inch doll might be a nice size.)
2. Dip the muslin in Elmer's glue to stiffen it and lay it on wax paper to dry, running your hands across the cloth to remove any excess glue.
3. Lift it and shape it to the body of the doll as desired. Let it dry.
4. Using a tacky white glue, and starting at the bottom of the skirt, glue little shells like periwinkles or limpets onto it in rows. To do this, dip the shell edges in glue and hold them in place for a while. You may wish to plan a pattern and have four rows of one kind of shell, four of another, and so on, or you may wish to have one kind of shell for the entire skirt and another kind for the waistband.
5. Make a simple muslin shirt in the same way — with Elmer's glue no sewing is needed. Simply shape the skirt and blouse to fit the doll. Let the material dry and glue on the shells.
6. For a hat, cut out a circle of fabric. Dip it in glue and fit it to the doll's head, over which you have laid a protective layer of Saran Wrap.
7. Cut out a circle of cardboard for the brim of the hat. Put it over the cloth circle on the doll's head and glue the excess cloth up under the hat brim. When the hat is dry, you can cut off the excess around the edge of the brim and you will have a neatly lined brim.
8. When the hat is dry, trim it with shells.
9. When all the shells are dry, brush them with Elmer's glue thinned with water or clear nail polish or spray them with a clear plastic spray to bring out the color of the shells. Decorate the dress and the hat with the thinnest possible pieces of grosgrain or silk ribbon (of a size used to decorate baby clothes).
10. Cut out a circle of wood to be a stand for the doll. Coat it with Elmer's glue and sprinkle sand on it.
11. Glue extra little shells onto it for decoration. Set the doll on it and place it under a glass dome.

Shell dolls were popular with collectors in the nineteenth century.
Below left: Shells from Africa were used by Carlos dos Santa Cruz of Lisbon,
Portugal, to make this lady and her parasol. Below right: Every shell has its use,
believes shell craftsman Carlos dos Santa Cruz. (Alison Shaw)

A Fish Rubbing

The youngster who catches his first fish can preserve it forever even if it isn't a sailfish worthy of mounting.

1. Wash it thoroughly but gently with liquid soap and water and dry it completely, making sure you don't injure the scales.
2. Cover the surface of a cookie sheet with water-base ink.
3. Lay the fish on a newspaper or a piece of oilcloth and gently roll it with the ink. Cover it completely.
4. Put a sheet of rice paper, or any other attractive paper, on top of it and rub the surface gently with your hands.
5. Peel the paper off carefully so it will not smudge. Leave the paper flat to dry (you may need to place a weight on it).

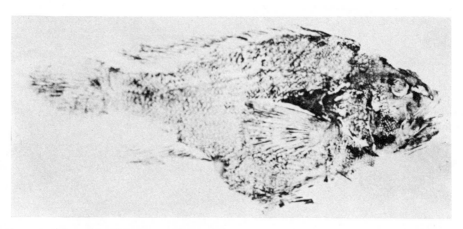

A fish rubbing will preserve a child's first catch forever.

Abalone Soup Bowls

Northern California abalone shells make fine snack dishes, with their attractive iridescent lining. The place to get them is about 50 yards from shore, and the person to get them is a scuba diver. When you have the abalone, remove the insides and leave the shell in the sun to dry. Cover the holes in the shell with masking tape applied to the back. Then apply Elmer's two-part epoxy to the inside. Let it dry and remove the tape.

Left: A sunporch coffee table can be made with a plywood base and a glass top the way Marianna McBride did for her seashore home. Right: Detail of McBride's coffee table.

 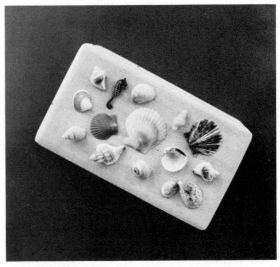

Dress up any plain wooden box with a design of shells.

This scallop shell chime on monofilament was the design of ten-year-old Scott Bettencourt.

95

Touch up the commonplace with shells the way Beth Meehan of Providence, Rhode Island, does.

A shell and a jewelry finding make this tie clip designed by Leighton Authier after a Connecticut shore holiday. (Alison Shaw)

An ocean-tumbled quahog shell with a leather thong through it works just fine as a ponytail holder.

Hawaiian memories were framed in this charming, old-fashioned way by Jane Farrow. (Peter Simon)

Below: This seashore memory box was designed on Martha's Vineyard by Doug Anderson and Alita Moyer. (Courtesy Alan-Mayhew Ltd., Vineyard Haven, Massachusetts)

5
Crafts from seaweed

All along the shore, seaweeds gather. Some cling to rocks and pilings. Some float free — pink, green, amber, and rust clumps that any beachcomber is sure to find if he goes exploring. And the vacationing craftsman can find a multitude of uses for it. Delicate, lacy seaweeds can give a personal touch to gift cards, bookmarks, or place cards. Seaweed can become a clump of grass, a hedge, a tree in an artist's painting. Paper marbleized using its jelly makes decorative book covers. Crinkly Irish moss found in tidepools or washed ashore is the base for that old-fashioned, nutritious pudding, blancmange (see page 152).

For years, Rose Treat lived in a house on the Massachusetts shore, and she watched the tide bring in strands and tufts and bouquets of many-colored seaweed. "I saw the seaweed drying on the rocks and the sand and the way it made pretty designs," she remembers. "And when I went into gift shops, I would see cards with seaweed on them, so I began to make my own." Now Rose Treat seaweed collages are sold in Boston art galleries, and her seaweed "notes" assure that her Christmas cards are distinctive each year.

Whenever she relaxes by taking a walk on the beach, Mrs. Treat makes sure she has a plastic bag with her. "And always a little stone to anchor it, so if you drop it, it won't blow away."

ROSE TREAT'S NOTEPAPER

The best seaweed to gather for notepaper is the delicate kind. Lacy Dasya pedicula, commonly known as chenille weed, is particularly good — it's a very fine pink, purple, or brown seaweed, almost as thin as grass.

Be sure that the seaweed you collect is in the water, not lying dried out along the shore. Fill your plastic bag with it and carry it home. Then fill a dishpan half full of cold water. Cut the paper to the size you want your notes to be. Water-color paper, which is thick, is good, or use Eaton's informals. If you have found a large clump of seaweed, you may want to cut it into smaller pieces, too.

Place one hand under the paper and hold it just beneath the surface of the water. With the other hand, lay the strands of seaweed on it one by one.

With a toothpick or knitting needle, position the seaweed in an attractive design. Then slowly lift the paper with the seaweed on it out of the water, tipping it slightly so as much water as possible drains off.

Lay the paper flat on a large white blotter or a kitchen or bath towel to dry. Depending upon climatic conditions and the thickness of the seaweed, this will take from 4 to 48 hours.

Lacy seaweed makes the most decorative notepaper.

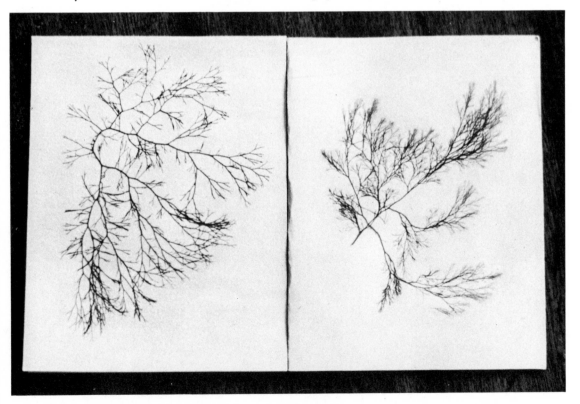

On days when she is feeling energetic and inspired, Rose Treat fashions collages from seaweed, but it is considerably more complicated than making notepaper.

For this she uses all-rag paper from a good art store. She fills a dozen basins with fresh water and puts the seaweed that she plans to use — heavier than that used for notepaper — into the basins, sorted according to shapes and shades. They must all be ready to put in place quickly on the floating paper.

She works in stages, perhaps applying one layer of seaweed one day and pressing it between two pieces of cloth-covered wallboard weighted down with rocks. "In the beginning, you have to go to it every few minutes to make sure the seaweed sticks to the paper, not to the cloth."

She may let one layer of her collage dry for several days. Then she sprinkles the paper lightly, but not long enough to dislodge the first layer, and applies a second layer. If you want to add still more seaweed, follow the same procedure until you achieve the effect you like.

This seaweed tree is the work of artist Ruth Bogan.

Marbleizing paper, using the gelatin from Irish moss as a base, is an unusual form of seaweed art. Irish moss is yellowish green or purplish and resembles little trees. It is found on most ocean beaches where there are rocks.

Marbleizing is a slightly more complex process than simply drifting seaweed onto papers and cards, but the entire family of Dr. Robert Blacklow of Chestnut Hill, Massachusetts, busily makes marbleized paper after a beach vacation. There is no rush. The moss will keep for months in a plastic bag in a cool, dark place.

"The gelatin in the Irish moss," says Winnie Blacklow, who is studying for a master's degree in biology at Wellesley College, "is a major source of carrageenin, which is used to thicken packaged puddings and Cool Whip and which is the medium for growing bacteria and fungi in the laboratory."

Materials

Irish moss
disposable roaster-size baking pans (12 x 16 inches)
newspaper
speedball or Grumbacher oil-based paints for block printing
plastic cups (not Styrofoam or waxed)
Clean Air solvent paint thinner
several 4-inch nails
Grumbacher or other high-quality drawing paper
wax paper
heavy books

1. Wash the Irish moss you have collected and dry it in the sun.
2. Take 1 cup of it, packed quite tightly, and put it into a kettle with 1 quart of water.
3. Boil it for 10 minutes.
4. Remove it from the heat and dilute the liquid with another quart of water. Let it sit overnight or for 12 hours, until it is the consistency of egg whites. (If by any chance you have collected the wrong seaweed, you will know it by the objectionable odor. Irish moss gelatin smells simply like the sea.)
5. At the egg-white-thick stage, stir it through a strainer into the roasting pan. Put what remains in the strainer back into the kettle with another quart of water to make a new batch. For that new batch,

Whether it's a dish of blancmange you want or some marbleized paper, crinkly Irish moss is the start of it.

Marbleizing paper is a family affair on Saturday mornings in the Blacklow home in Chestnut Hill, Massachusetts. Here, egg-white-thick seaweed jelly is poured through a strainer at the start of the process.

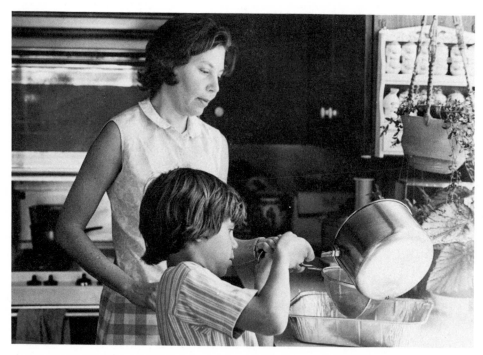

Opposite page: (a) A roasting pan is the right-sized container for marbleizing. (b) Nails are used to dot the jelly with oil-based paint. (c) Once the paint dots have been applied, they must be swirled into a pattern. (d) To prevent air bubbles from forming, the paper should be smoothed as it is laid on the gelatin surface. (e) When the paper is lifted from the seaweed gelatin, the colors come, too. (f) The finished product, marbleized paper, can be used as gift wrapping, bookmarks, book covers, or to decorate boxes.

a

b

c

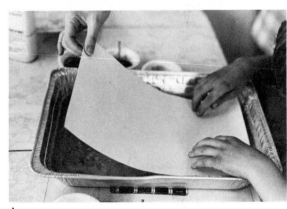

d

e

f

you will probably not have to dilute the liquid after cooking, for enough of the gelatinous substance will have been removed in the first cooking.

6. The substance in the roasting pan is your printing medium. With a piece of newspaper, try to blot up all the air bubbles, for wherever there is a bubble, no ink will reach the paper.

7. When the jelly appears smooth, squeeze about 1 1/2 inches of paint into each plastic cup you will be using and add 1 tablespoon of solvent to each. Stir with a builder's nail to the consistency of mustard.

8. Dot the surface of the jelly with spots of paint. (You can use the nails for this purpose, too.) Make one row of one color, one of another. Cover almost the entire surface with the tiny dots. Then cut through the dots with one of the nails — but not deeply. Swish the colors up and down to make a feather or herringbone pattern.

9. Cut your paper to the size of the pan and lay it on the surface of the jelly. To prevent air bubbles from forming, start laying the paper in one corner, resting and smoothing it down as you go, either from left to right or right to left. Be sure not to wait longer than 3 minutes from the time you apply the dots until the time you put down the paper.

10. Gently press the paper down for about 5 seconds.

11. Raise it, brushing off all the excess jelly into the pan with your hand. Rinse the paper thoroughly in warm or cold water, gently rubbing the gel off the surface of the paper.

12. Lay the printed sheet flat on newspaper (not too close to any heat) to dry.

13. When the paper is bone dry, remove it from the newspaper. Put it between two sheets of wax paper and pile heavy books on it. Leave the paper under the books overnight or until it is nice and smooth and flat.

14. Meanwhile, clean the jelly that remains in the roasting pan by laying newspaper cut to size on top of it. When you remove it, you will remove the leftover dabs of color, too. Either fresh or used jelly will keep in the refrigerator for about a week. When it is removed, it should be left out until it is about 70 degrees before you print with it again.

Use your marbleized paper for bookmarks, notepad covers, or for decorative covers for address books or bridge tally pads.

6
Gold, gems, and minerals

For the vacation craftsperson who knows where to look for it, there is still "gold in them thar hills" — and rubies and sapphires, amethysts, garnets, quartz, and other semiprecious stones. One of the richest gem states, with more than three hundred minerals, is North Carolina, which is rich, too, in the scenery that makes for a popular vacation place. Both the Great Smokies and the Blue Ridge mountains rise in North Carolina.

In the spring, they are a blaze of pink and orange azaleas. And the snow white of dogwood gleams in the green forests. Then laurel and rhododendron blossom. And in the fall, the mountains are scarlet with maples and gold with tulip trees against the pines. The air is so fresh, "you think you're in another world sometimes," one old-timer, Blaine Blackburn of Flat Rock, puts it. "There's just two things I want to do up here — go along a stream and trout-fish a couple of hours and then mineral-hunt."

The fish are an immediate satisfaction, dipped in cornmeal and fried in deep, hot fat for supper. "But the minerals are permanent. They can be passed down from generation to generation. You can keep them the way they are or do all sorts of things with them. If you get a good stone, you can make a pendant. All you need is a neck chain and a bell cap from a jewelry findings store or a crafts shop. You can cement the cap onto the stone as is, or you can polish it, file away a little rough spot so the surface will hold glue, and then put the cap and chain on," Mr. Blackburn says.

To polish the stones you need a tumbler or a vibrasonic tumbler. With the former, which can be purchased for under $50, it takes three weeks of tumbling to get the stone you wish. With the latter, which costs $100 to $300, the same work can be done in three days.

Mr. Blackburn runs the Rag Doll Craft Shop in Flat Rock now, and does a lot of gemcutting, but for years, gems were just a hobby with him, and he likes to advise others about rock collecting.

"You're on vacation in the mountains," he notes, "and if you keep your eyes out for rocks around here, there are so many pretty ones you just can't miss. Just around Spruce Pine here there are ten or fifteen places to look. There's white quartz sometimes with pink feldspar in it. You can make beautiful bookends of a conglomerate like that. Why, some of the stuff we see here is just out of this world, it's so lovely. We even have gold if you want it."

Throughout the South and in much of the West, if you have neither the time nor the knowledge to go rock hunting without guidance but like the idea of the hunt, there are mines open to the public for a fee. For $3 or $4, you can buy a bucket of gravel and find what you will find. You can either take your bucketful home to sift through or examine it on the spot to see if you have gems in among the dirt and stones.

"A boy went over to the Yukon Mine one day and bought twenty-eight bucketsful. But they were worth it. He found he had a sapphire that weighed 566 carats — which is tremendous — it was one of the prettiest sapphires I've ever seen. Of course, lots of times you don't find anything precious, but it's fun anyway," Mr. Blackburn adds.

In many states where there are minerals, local Chambers of Commerce will supply maps showing the location of mines that allow do-it-yourself digging. Periodicals like *Rock and Gem* and *Gems and Minerals* also tell you where you can find what. In West Virginia you can dig coal and make it into jewelry. You can usually rent a shovel, a prospector's pick (a combination hammer and pick), and a chisel, or you can take along your own.

You can make bracelets in the same general way as pendants. An attractive rock can be taken to a rock shop to be split and polished to make into bookends. Or you can attach clock works, available at many rock shops to the polished face.

A few years ago, Marion Lillie of Bay View, Idaho, was visiting in Clear Lake County, California, north of San Francisco. There she found quartz crystals shining like diamonds on the ground where they had been kicked up by a deer. She gathered some from under the ponderosa pines and used the best to make a mobile. Here are her directions:

GEM MOBILE

Materials

epoxy
bell caps
gems
one 8-inch, 24-gauge wire
one 10-inch, 24-gauge wire
one 18-inch, 24-gauge wire
nylon fishing line
one swivel from a fishing leader, small size, including clasp

1. With epoxy, cement the bell caps to the gems and let them set for several days.

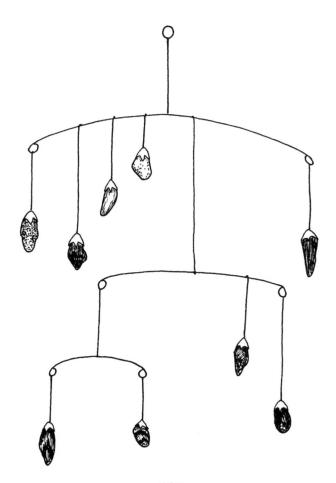

2. Start with the shortest wire, which will become the bottom wire of your mobile. Curl the ends of it into loops.
3. Tie an 8-inch piece of fishing line to one gem, a 9-inch piece to another, and suspend them from the ends of the wire. Use a fisherman's knot and a spot of glue to make sure the line holds, or put a match to it so the two ends of the plastic line melt together.
4. To find the balance point for your first wire, hold it on your finger somewhere near the center. When you have found the spot, tie and glue on a 4-inch piece of fishing line at that point.
5. Make curls in the ends of the 10-inch wire.
6. Tie and glue the unattached end of the 4-inch line to one end of the 10-inch wire.
7. Hang more gems on the other end of the wire. These should be selected to balance the weight of the gems on the bottom wire.
8. Now hold the 10-inch wire on your finger somewhere near the middle, and balance it again. At the balance point, tie about 14 inches of fish line.
9. At the unattached end of the fish line, tie the 18-inch wire (bend its two ends as you did the ends of the other two wires to form a curl).
10. Suspend more gems from the ends of that wire, again balancing both sides of the mobile. Hang the gems on lines of varying lengths.
11. Balance the 18-inch wire with the 10- and 8-inch wires below it from your finger. When you find the center, tie on a shorter piece of fishing line and the leader. Remember that, in making a mobile, balance and imagination are the important ingredients. If you have no gemstones, beach glass, pretty varnished pebbles, or slices of rock may be used instead.

WALL PLAQUES

Tumbled gems may also be glued onto glass in a pretty pattern with epoxy and framed with liquid solder. Just remember that if you have polished a stone or gem, its surface must be "roughed up" with a knife sharpener, file, or silicon carbide paper from a hardware store (used with water as a moistener). If you don't do this, the glue will not hold.

PAPERWEIGHTS

Of course, split stones or geodes — stones wth a cavity in them lined with crystals — will make handsome paperweights. If you don't have your own stonecutter, most rock shop proprietors will be accommodating about cutting your favorite stone for you — or slicing it, if that suits your purpose better. Geodes that have been split are also good for bookends.

Geodes and a root are vacation mementos for Hildegarde Ruof of Freiburg, Germany.

These geode bookends were split at the Roc Shop in Edgartown, Massachusetts.

Pretty gems combined with copper jeweler's wire can make a decorative "tree" or floral "bouquet."

GEM TREES

If you have pretty gems, twist copper jeweler's wire around them, attach the wires to a piece of driftwood or a rock, and construct an artificial bonsai for your mantelpiece.

A Gold Bauble

Now that the federal government, after a forty-year prohibition, is allowing individual citizens to buy, sell, and own gold without having to acquire a license, it's gold-panning time again. Alaska, Arizona, California, Colorado, Idaho, Montana, Nevada, New Mexico, Oregon, Utah, Washington, Wyoming — vacation in any one of these states and you may find gold. All you need are directions from a local Chamber of Commerce or a rock shop and a pan that will cost you up to $3. Most rock shops sell them.

Then take a walk along the mountain stream to which you have been directed and see what you will see, or go to an area that has been seeded with gold, where you will pay a fee, but where there is sure to be gold to gather in your pan. Beware of prospecting on state or national land (except forests), Indian reservations, or military installations. You may, however, prospect in general in lands managed by the Bureau of Land Management. If you have no mechanical equipment, you need no permit. When and if you have your gold dust or gold nugget, you can buy a clear glass bubble to put it in at a rock shop and hang it around your neck or attach it to a key chain. Or you can get two bubbles and make cuff links.

Gold Art

In Lewiston, Idaho, in the Elk City mining district, Mr. and Mrs. Ernest Butler operate their own rock shop. They suggest that if you get enough gold nuggets on your travels, you might want to preserve them by "painting" a picture with them. Use a velour paper and attach the nuggets and gold dust with Elmer's glue. Have the design clearly in mind before you start applying your gold, for the glue will dry quickly. Mrs. Butler has made animal, plant, and landscape paintings with the gold she has collected.

7
Pebbles, glass, rocks, and fossils

What vacationer can resist picking up just one more beautifully colored pebble or handsome rock or delicately colored, water-smoothed bit of beach glass? And who doesn't have boxes of these treasures stored in a closet, wondering what he thought he'd do with them? Here — for the collections you already have or the treasures you pick up on your next trip — are some imaginative ways to transform them into craft projects.

A marble box becomes much more when polished stones are glued to the top.

Beach Stone Jewelry

Polished beach stones make handsome jewelry. They are best gathered a little below high tide, for when they are wet you can see their colors best. Take them home and tumble them in a rock tumbler until they gleam. Just remember that whatever their shape is when they go into the tumbler, will be their shape when the tumbling is done. To change shape, they must be ground with emery.

After you have found a pretty stone and tumbled it, roughen the area onto which you will glue a bell cap or ring or whatever other finding seems appropriate, and, with Duro clear epoxy, attach the finding to the stone. Before you wear the stone, be sure that the glue is completely dry.

Tumbled beach stones make handsome jewelry, like these pieces designed by Jane Farrow.

This beach-stone necklace is rich in memories.

Pebbles, polished or unpolished, may be used as coffee table tops. On a visit to Greece a few years ago, Pearl Braude of Providence, Rhode Island, walked along the Aegean and collected little gray and white, black and brown, and red and yellow pebbles. With clear epoxy, she glued a pattern of pebbles, all about the same size and depth, onto a wooden coffee table top. She then sprayed them with Duco clear spray varnish to give them a sheen. If you prefer, leave the stones plain for a casual and rustic look.

If you are an indefatigable beach pebble collector, you can have a table designed with a recess in the top and glass over it through which you can see your treasures. Ted Farrow of Chilmark, Massachusetts, designed just such a table for his wife, Jane. When she tires of the assortment of stones on top of the pile, she lifts up the glass, stirs them up, and instantly has a new design of colors and shapes to enjoy.

All you have to do to change the design of this table made by Ted Farrow is to take off the glass and stir up the pebbles. (Peter Simon)

Pebbles from an Aegean beach were turned into a mosaic on a Hans Knoll table by Rhode Islander Pearl Braude. (Dick Benjamin)

By far the easiest way to transform stones and pebbles into vacation memorabilia — especially for children — is to glue together two or more stones that suggest a shape to you. Then paint them with acrylics, household paint, tempera, oil, or poster paint. If you use poster paint, you must seal the rock first with shellac or a clear spray so the paint will stay.

To make faces or to write messages on your rocks, use a felt-tipped pen and permanent ink. Be sure any glaze or spray you have used is dry before you begin.

With a little imagination, small stones may be turned into perky bugs, saucy flat-footed people, or turtles. Rock critters have, indeed, more personality than an undecorated Pet Rock — and they don't cost anything, either.

These perky little people were fashioned on an island holiday by the Lightfoot children of Guilford, Connecticut.

Soulful critters like these created by Karen Bailey of Oak Ridge, Tennessee, can be modeled of clay or made from painted pebbles.

Rocks collected on a holiday in Maine were painted by Susan Wilson of Ohio. (Joan Noone)

Painting rocks is a nice vacation hobby for children. These were done by Susan, Lynne, and Lori Robertson. (Lawrence S. Millard)

Rock Doorstops

Many a painted rock has found its use as a doorstop, glibly painted with a saying like DON'T TREAD ON ME or DON'T TURN ME OVER, or with a footprint painted on it. If you prefer rock decorations to be pretty rather than funny, paint floral designs on your rocks.

Weed Pots

Visitors to the mountains might take along a knapsack to collect the pretty pebbles and then use them to make weed pots. Creek and river beds are particularly good places to find pebbles. One indefatigable hiker and collector says that the best she has found are in Jackson County in western North Carolina, along the wild and scenic Chattooga River, where both quartz and mica abound. She gathers pebbles that are about 1/2 inch in diameter, and when she gets home, she glues them to bottles.

To do this you should have a square- or rectangular-based bottle (William's Lectric Pre-shave preparation is an ideal shape). Remove the label, wash and dry the bottle, and cut off the top with a glass cutter. File the rough edge with a file or with a coarse emery board so it will not cut you. Coat the bottle with Elmer's glue and sift sand onto the glue and let it dry. When you are sure it has dried, start gluing your larger pebbles around the bottle. Let them dry and then fill in the spaces with smaller pebbles. Either leave them as they are or spray-varnish them.

116

Left: A menorah made of Israeli beach glass mounted in aluminum. (Henny Wenkart) Right: Fourteen-year-old Ted Howes of King of Prussia, Pennsylvania, collected this beach glass on a New England holiday. (Mark Lennihan)

A BEACH GLASS MENORAH

A few years ago, when Henry Epstein of Cambridge and New York was beachcombing near Caeserea in Israel, he found dark green and blue and white beach glass. He combined it with red and gold and brown street glass collected in New York and tumbled with sand in his tumbler. "You just can't get all the colors you want on beaches," he explains. "That's why I sometimes pick up bright-colored bits of glass I find in city streets."

He decided that since much of his glass had come from Israel, he would display the collection in a menorah. Ideally, he would have liked to use a piece of olive wood as his base, but lacking that, he made it of polished heavy sheet aluminum that can be cut with shears. He formed the menorah and cut a freeform window in it for displaying the glass. Then he glued the glass in place near the edge of the "window" with 5-minute epoxy. "Use your imagination. Make a sculpture with your glass," he says.

117

Top left: Even a few pieces of beach glass can make a seashore souvenir. This sailboat picture was made by eight-year-old Leslie Labis and her seven-year-old brother, John. Bottom left: Long ago, Indians painted their faces with the yellow ocher pigment found in chunks of ciderite. Indian paint pots found on the beach today have lost their pigment. If you find one, the hole where the pigment was. makes a nice mounting for beach glass. Right: Sea glass, cork, and monofilament make this multicolored mobile. (Joan Noone)

A BEACH GLASS SCULPTURE

If aluminum seems too hard to deal with, glue three or four shingles together, back to back, so you have a thickness of about 1 inch. With a coping saw, jigsaw, or pocketknife, cut a "window" in which to frame your glass. Before you insert the glass, however, weather the window so it matches the rest of the shingle by leaving it out in the salt air for a week or two. Then glue in pretty pieces of glass, attach a monofilament fish line to the shingles, and hang your "sculpture" in a dark corridor through which light comes from both ends. This isn't quite a mobile, but it makes a handsome decoration.

ROCKS AND PLANTS

Wherever slate quarries are located, there are always shops selling slate boxes and penholders and bookends, but rough pieces of slate can also be most effective household decorations. If you bring back a slice or two of slate from your vacation, simply break it with a hammer into interesting shapes. Then use it as the base for a dried floral arrangement. Pearly everlasting, goldenrod, milkweed pods, moss, driftwood — all go well with it. Set the flowers in with window sealer, which comes in long strips and can be camouflaged with moss, or Sahara Floral Oasis from a florist's. If you work skillfully, you can also use clear epoxy. If you use moss in a rock and plant arrangement, be sure to air-dry it before you attach it. Lay the moss on a box with a screen top to get air underneath it or leave it for a while on the furnace. If it loses color during this process, you can spray it before mounting it with olive green floral spray.

You needn't only use slate, of course, in a rock arrangement. It can be Georgia or New Hampshire granite, Kentucky limestone, or Montana onyx. Limestone often has natural holes that can be used as containers for dried plants or flowers. And one traveler to China, Marylin Chou of Yorktown Heights, New York, recently brought back from her journey miniature rocks from Kweilin, in southern China. Their full-size counterparts were the inspiration for much early Chinese landscape painting. She had a ceramic tray designed to go with the rocks. Then she put water into the tray and set about recreating, as nearly as possible, the landscape she had seen. She found miniature weeds, for example, resembling weeds she had seen in China, and she planted them, with some of the soil on their roots, in crevices in the rocks. An indoor rock garden, she believes, should simulate an outdoor landscape.

TERRARIUMS

If you have had a woodland vacation, you might wish to remember it with some mossy stones and forest plants laid on the "land" of your terrarium. (Terrarium land should consist of a layer of gravel, some charcoal, and a top layer of sterile soil from a nursery in which you place your plants and onto which you lay the stones for your landscape.) A good terrarium container is an aquarium with a cover on it to keep the moisture in. If you've been on a desert holiday, desert sand and rocks and cactus (probably purchased — there are few kinds you can dig up) do nicely in terrariums, too. Be sure not to cover a desert terrarium.

119

FOSSILS

Although in many areas you will find that fossil collecting is taboo, there are other places where bringing home a reasonable number of fossils is allowed. If you are going on public land to hunt fossils, be sure to check with the local Bureau of Land Management office to see what the rules and regulations are. Fossils are frequently found in road cuts and at construction sites and quarries. They may be in rocks made of mud, sand, and pebbles, and occasionally they are found in marble or slate and sometimes in volcanic ash. Sometimes they are found along beaches. U.S. Geological Survey maps will help you to find them, as will various rockhound publications. Some fossils are encased in rocks and require the hand of a specialist to split the rock and expose the fossil. Others — along the shore, for example — are imprints of tiny fish, sharks' teeth, shells, and skeletons of fish that can be clearly seen. Since a fossil is rare and precious and delicate, most collectors simply display them as is — perhaps under glass in a coffee table — rather than trying to transform them into something else.

ARROWHEADS

If you are vacationing where Indians have lived and earth is turned for farming, or a windstorm has just blown the topsoil off the fields, perhaps you will find arrowheads. Like fossils, they are best simply displayed, without embellishment, on a mantel or against an attractive background in a glass-topped coffee table.

The arrowheads he finds in fields after a storm are turned into a coffee table by Herbert R. Hancock.

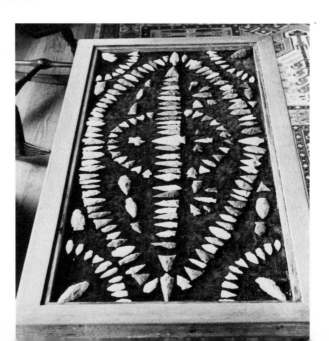

8
Baskets

Almost any country vacation offers a variety of materials for making baskets — pine needles from the woods, honeysuckle from the fields. If you are at the beach, you can even weave a little seaweed in with the honeysuckle. Basketry is one of the oldest crafts there is, and how much pleasanter to weave your own on a sunny shore or a cool wood than to buy one in a hot basket market by the roadside!

PINE NEEDLE BASKETS

Native to the Deep South is the long-leaf pine, tall and willowy with needles up to 18 inches long. Nancy Grant of Oak Ridge, Tennessee, has learned how to fashion its needles into baskets, making especially handsome patterns by also weaving light-colored natural raffia into her designs. Here are her instructions:

1. Arrange the pine needles into bundles 1 to 2 inches in diameter. Remove the sheaths and tie each bundle together with a rubber band.

Long-leaf pine and raffia are the ingredients for a pine needle basket.

2. Put 1 teaspoon of dish detergent into a shallow sink of lukewarm water. Add the pine needle bundles and wash them. The bundles should be rather loose so you can rub the needles back and forth between your hands.
3. Spread the needles out on a sheet outdoors in the shade to dry. This will take about a day.
4. Retie them into bundles of seven. Now they are ready to work with.
5. Take a macramé ring 1 1/2 inches in diameter. Wrap the ring with raw raffia, using the double buttonhole stitch and a blunt-ended tapestry needle. When the ring is entirely covered, weave in the loose end and cut it off.
6. Tie a second strand of raffia to one side of the ring (try to conceal the knot as well as possible). Stretch the second strand across the ring and insert it into an inside stitch of the raffia on the opposite side of the ring. Insert the needle into the next stitch on that side and come back to the opposite side of the ring with the raffia. Continue this procedure until you have woven twelve raffia spokes across the ring in an over-and-under way. When you are finished, make a slip knot under one side of the ring and cut the raffia off. This is the center of the bottom of your basket.
7. Now take one of the bundles of seven pine needle clusters (without the rubber band around them, of course). Sew the needles to the ring with a strand of raffia, using the overcast stitch. By the time you get to the end of two rows, you will probably be short a needle, for some needles are longer than others. Add another, so that at all times you are binding on seven needles.
8. To make a shallow bowl, bind the needles on flat — as if you were making a hot plate — for nine rows. Then turn the bundle of needles up and begin to construct the sides in exactly the same way that you have the bottom, binding the needles on with raffia, using the overcast stitch. If your raffia thread runs out, tie another one onto the end of it, concealing it under the needles as well as possible.
9. The sides of the basket should be five or six rows high. Then to make the rim of the basket, bind two to three rows alongside the top row.
10. To finish off the basket, taper ends of the needles with a scissors and backstitch with the raffia into the previous stitch. Don't make a knot at the end or it will show.
11. Spray the basket with shellac if you choose or leave it natural. These baskets may be washed in detergent and lukewarm water, but dry them quickly (though not in a hot place) or they will mildew.

Top: The overcast stitch is a basic one in pine needle basketry. Right: Nancy Grant's basket. Left: A long-leaf pine needle medallion. (Robert McCrystal)

If you don't feel quite ambitious enough to make a whole basket, simply combine raffia and pine needles around a macramé ring to make a pendant. Hang it around your neck with a leather thong.

In the spring and summer, the fragrance of honeysuckle perfumes the air in many vacation spots. The flowers are flavorful to suck on as you amble through fields and clearings, but the vines can be a long-lasting part of your house if you turn them into a basket the way Mara Cary of Nantucket, author of *Basic Baskets* and *Useful Baskets*, does.

1. Steam the honeysuckle vine. For a 7-inch-high, 28-inch-round, 9-inch-diameter basket, you will need forty-two pieces of yard-long honeysuckle and fifteen pieces that are 2 yards long.
2. Steam five or six pieces at a time by coiling them together and stuffing them into an old pail or kettle. Place weights on them and half-fill the kettle with water.
3. If the water evaporates during the cooking, be sure to replenish it. Simmer for about 4 hours. Cool and rinse the coils. Spread them out or hang them up to dry. They can then be stored indefinitely until you want to use them. Then simply soak them for 5 to 10 minutes in water.

Here are Mrs. Cary's directions as she explained them to me:

Materials

42 pieces of honeysuckle, 1 yard long
15 pieces, longer (2 yards or so)

I am having you cut them too long, so you'll trim them later. And you probably have more long pieces than you need, but that's better than too few. You really *will* need the forty-two shorter ones.

1. Divide the forty-two shorter pieces into groups of six and weave them into a mat. Try to make the woven mat more or less in the center of the pieces. Use clothespins to help hold it.
2. Take the first longer piece and weave in and out around the "mat."
3. When you've gone once around, divide your *first* (and only the first) group of six into two groups of three. This will allow you to continue weaving in and out.
4. After about four rounds, begin to shape up the sides. You do this by holding each stake in the position you want it as you weave. Pull the weaver snug. Also, you can sort of think of keeping the stakes close together.

Weave the shorter pieces of honeysuckle into a mat. Weave a longer piece in and around the mat. Divide the first group of six into two groups of three. Start to shape the sides of the basket. Two or three stoutish pieces of honeysuckle will make your handle. To be used as a planter, a finished honeysuckle basket should be suspended by strong twine. (Mara Cary)

5. As you weave up the sides (I sometimes used three or four weavers at once), have fun. Arrange your seaweed here and there and highlight it with a shell.
6. Do at least four rounds of plain weaving at the top to get the stakes back in order and to do the border upon.
7. The border: Use each group of six (or three) as one. Begin anywhere and proceed in either direction. Take the first one to the outside of the one next to it, inside the next, and back to the outside of the third one over. Do *not* pull this one tight. Leave it arched, as you will be filling in the space with the final ones. You can pull them tighter once you've made the border.
8. The handle: Use two or three stoutish long pieces (they must arch at least three times across). Stick the ends down into the weaving on the side of the basket. Arch them over the basket and decide the best shape for the arch. Thread them *through* the side of the basket (at the opposite point) anywhere *below* the border. Then wrap them five or so times around the first arch back to the starting point. Thread them through on that side and wrap back to the opposite side. You can wrap the same slant as before or make a crisscross slant. Here you cut them off long enough to slip down into the weaving.
9. Or the sling: three pieces of twine about 1 1/2 yards long. Tie a knot in one end. Thread one up through each of three more or less equidistant spaces in the bottom of basket. Then thread them back to the outside, just below the border. Gather the ends together and put in another knot. If you want to use it as a planter be sure to have strong twine.

9
Natural dyes

If you weave, spin, or hook your own rugs, a vacation in the country in late summer or early fall provides a wonderful opportunity to make your own dyes. If you don't like sassafras tea or pokeberry wine, if hickory nuts stick in your teeth and a dried goldenrod arrangement would clash with your décor, think about using those plants for their dyes. Sassafras roots give a pink shade; hickory nuts, a gray; bayberry, a tan; pokeberry and sumac, a deep red dye. The dye from Queen Anne's lace or acorns is greenish; the dye from the bark of the oak tree is tan.

Sophie Block of West Tisbury, Massachusetts, makes her own bread in a wall oven beside her eighteenth-century fireplace. Surrounded by that fragrant smell, she spins wool from a neighbor's sheep on a hand spindle and then stirs up enamel kettles of dye. Goldenrod is one of the dyes she finds most effective. "You can get all kinds of golds and bright yellows from different varieties," she says.

If you dye raw wool, it must be washed in hot, soapy water several times until the lanolin is out or it will not take the dye. Let it cool to lukewarm in the rinse water. Wool should be handled very gently and should never be subjected to great changes of temperature. If you use a lukewarm mordant to set the dye, use a lukewarm dye bath. Unless otherwise specified, use an enamel or porcelain pot for all processes. Always mordant and dye the wool when it is wet.

And when you dry wool, be careful. Dry it indoors or outdoors in the shade, after gently squeezing out some of the water but not wringing the wool. A dish rack or a rack made of chicken wire so the air gets underneath it is especially good.

Although there are many exacting aspects to dyeing, it is not an altogether perfect art. The many recipes for dyes vary, and you can play a little yourself with the dyeing process. If you have no alum or chrome to use as a mordant, for example, but do have a potful of potatoes cooking on the stove, try the potato water as a mordant. It can make an effective substitute.

GOLDENROD DYE

1. For the mordant, you will need 1/2 ounce of chrome (potassium dichromate). Be sure to wear rubber gloves while using it and to wash thoroughly any utensils involved in the dyeing process (unless, of course, you keep them for dyeing only), for most mordants are poisonous. Dissolve the chrome in 4 to 4 1/2 gallons of soft cold water. (If you don't have soft water you can use rainwater.) Immerse the washed, wet wool. Gradually bring it to a simmer, and simmer for 1 hour. If the water boils away, keep adding more so the amount remains constant. Allow the wool to cool in the mordant. Rinse it before adding it to the dye.
2. For the dye, you will need 1 peck of fresh flower heads and 4 gallons of water for 1 pound of wool. Pick the flowers just as they are coming into bloom. Take them from the stems and soak them in the 4 gallons of cold water overnight.
3. In the morning, simmer them for 1 hour and strain out the flowers. The liquid that remains is your dye bath. Allow it to cool. Then add the wet, mordanted wool.
4. Bring the bath to a simmer slowly and let it simmer for 30 minutes to an hour, until the wool is the shade you wish. Allow the wool to cool in the bath.
5. Rinse the wool gently in cool water until the water runs clear.
6. Dry the wool.

BAYBERRY DYE

1. For the mordant, you will need 1 ounce of alum (1 1/2 tablespoons) to 1/4 pound of wool and 1 gallon of cold water. Add the alum to the water and dissolve it. Add the wet washed wool and simmer it for 1 hour. Let it cool in the mordant. Rinse it well before dyeing.
2. For the dye you will need 2 pounds of bayberry leaves and 1 gallon of water. Macerate the leaves and let them soak overnight in the gallon of cold water. In the morning, simmer them for 2 hours and strain them. Cool the water. This is the dye bath.

128

3. Add the wool, washed and mordanted. Bring it to a simmer and let it simmer for about 30 minutes until it is the desired color. Allow it to cool in the dye.
4. Rinse it well and dry it.

POKEBERRY DYE

For this dye, vinegar serves as the mordant and is also the liquid in which you cook the berries. This makes a very pretty dye, but not a long-lasting one. Exposure to the light will make it fade in a matter of months.

  1 pound pokeberries
  1 gallon liquid, half water, half vinegar
  a tin or enamel pot (tin will give an exceptionally bright color)
  1/4 pound wool

1. Soak the berries in the water-vinegar mixture overnight in the enamel or tin pot. The next day, simmer them for 1 hour.
2. Strain the mixture; the liquid that remains is the dye.
3. Add the wet washed wool and bring it to a simmer. Simmer it until it is the desired shade (about 30 minutes).
4. Cool the wool in the water; rinse it well and dry it.

BLACK WALNUT DYE

No mordant is needed for this dye.

  1/4 peck green hulls from black walnuts
  4 to 4 1/2 gallons of water
  1 pound wool

1. Soak the hulls, lacerated or cut from the nuts, in water overnight.
2. The next day, simmer them for several hours.
3. Strain out the hulls. This remaining liquid is the dye bath. Let it cool to lukewarm.
4. Put the washed wet wool in the dye. Heat it to the simmering point and let it continue to simmer until the wool is the desired shade.
5. Rinse the wool thoroughly and dry it.

10
Paper making

Here's an interesting project for one of those days when the weather isn't nice enough to go to the beach. Making your own paper requires a few materials and some preparation — not much — but if you have the materials on hand, that rainy day could turn out to be one of the highlights of your vacation.

Elaine Koretsky of Brookline, Massachusetts, travels extensively, often in exotic places, and she is likely to come home with a Hawaiian banana plant or an agave from Greece, which she transforms into textured paper. She has a plant importer's license, but you don't have to go abroad to find the makings of your own souvenir paper. The leaves and stalks of wild iris, cattails, and Queen Anne's lace are all good materials. You can even press the petals of wild flowers or a sprig of seaweed into your paper, so collect some of these, too.

Materials

enough wild iris stalks and leaves, cattail stalks and leaves, or Queen Anne's lace stalks and leaves to fill a large pot one-third full
a large enamel or stainless steel pot
4 quarts water
1 teaspoon lye
an old blender or a mortar and pestle
a Styrofoam ice cooler (rectangular)
cheesecloth
a wooden frame with window screening stretched across and nailed to it
small pieces of sheet or old wool blanket (the size of the paper you wish to make)
two pieces of plywood as large as your paper
weights (encyclopedias or other heavy books will do)

Jars of leaves for paper-making
fill Elaine Koretsky's studio.

1. Fill the pot a third full with the plant material you have collected.
2. Add as much water as you need to cover it.
3. Wearing rubber gloves, stir in the lye. (If you have not used 4 quarts of water, reduce the amount of lye accordingly.)
4. Cook this mixture until it is mushy, from 20 to 30 minutes.
5. Drain the water off and rinse the pulp thoroughly (wear rubber gloves again) to remove all the lye.
6. A handful at a time, put the plant material into the blender. Fill it with water and blend it until it becomes a pulp, or pound it in the mortar and pestle to pulp consistency, or both. When this process is done, the individual fibers should barely be seen.
7. Strain the water out through cheesecloth. You should have a medium-sized jar of pulp.
8. Put the pulp in the cooler and add eight times as much water as you have pulp. (Should you want thinner paper after you have experimented a little, use less pulp.)
9. Keep the pulp mixture stirred up or it will be unevenly distributed. But if you want to add some chopped-up flower petals for texture, do. They need not be cooked.

10. Slide the framed screen under the water and lift it straight up.
11. Turn the screen face down on the pieces of blanket or sheeting that you have laid on one of the pieces of plywood.
12. Sponge the excess water from the back of the screen and lift it up. The sheet of paper should fall off onto the cloth.
13. Make more sheets, following the same process. Lay all the sheets on top of each other, but with the cloth pieces separating them. End with a piece of cloth on top. Lay the second plywood board on the last piece of cloth.
14. Pile heavy books on top and leave the paper under pressure for half an hour.
15. Remove each piece of paper from its cloth backing (called "felt") and iron it thoroughly dry with a hot iron at the cotton setting. If your paper has not set, you can go back to the cooler stage, adding to the pulp a little discarded writing paper that you have chopped up in your blender.
16. If you want to press a whole flower or seaweed into the paper, lay the flower or seaweed between two sheets of thin paper on your ironing board and iron them together.

A wooden frame with window screening stretched across it is the form for making the sheets of paper.

Above: Out of the cooler comes a sheet of paper.

Below: Banana and red seaweed were the base of this paper. (Samuel Koretsky)

11
Dolls

In the Appalachians, apple-doll carving is an old-time craft. But since apples grow wild and in orchards in many parts of the country, this craft is one that many vacationers can enjoy. If you don't see wild apples, many orchards nowadays invite you to come in and pick your own for so much a bushel. If the apples you pick are firm, hard ones like Winesaps or Jonathans or Golden Delicious, use a few you don't feel like eating for apple dolls.

Nelda White of Oak Ridge, Tennessee, offers this authentic Appalachian recipe:

APPLE DOLLS

Materials

apples, about 3 inches in diameter
pocketknife or toothpicks
lemon juice
salt
sharpened sticks or dowels
lamb's wool
Elmer's glue or Sobo
needlenose pliers
18-gauge wire
crafts shop clay
cotton batting and nylon hose
doll clothes
bead or seed eyes

Character is the quality Nelda White seeks in making her Appalachian apple dolls.

1. Peel the apple.
2. With a pocketknife, cut down for a forehead, shape a nose, and make slits for the eyes and mouth. Cut the ears. Remember not to cut too deeply into the head of an apple doll. A little goes a long way when the apple dries. You may even prefer to do much of your drawing of the features with a toothpick rather than a knife for this reason. Making good apple dolls takes practice.

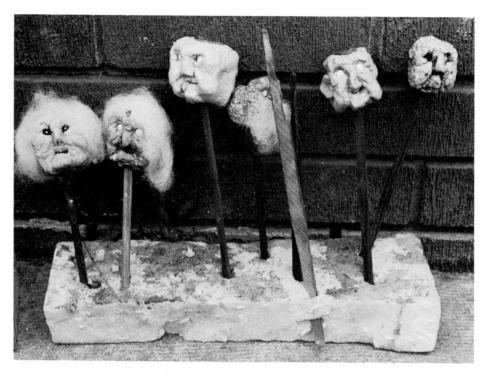

Heads must be dried on dowels or sticks for five to six weeks.

3. Dip the head in lemon juice and sprinkle it with salt. This will keep the doll from darkening after it dries.
4. Put the head on a dowel or stick and set it upright in the sun to dry. This will take five to six weeks, if the weather is sunny and dry.
5. While the doll is drying, pull the ears and nose out now and then to shape them a bit. At about four weeks, insert the bead or seed eyes.
6. You will know when the head is ready by its leathery feeling. Glue lamb's wool hair on with Elmer's or Sobo.
7. With the needlenose pliers and the wire, fashion a stick body. Model the feet and hands of clay. Mold them onto the legs and arms and bake in a 300-degree oven for 25 minutes or until brown.
8. Wrap the body and legs and arms in the cotton batting and nylon and dress. Place the eyes. Mrs. White favors hillbilly types. In any case, the faces you end up with will be wizened old faces with many wrinkles, so dress the dolls accordingly. "What's fun about an apple doll," says Mrs. White "is that you get a different face every time."

A farm vacation might mean that there were cornhusks available to make flowers or dolls or wreaths with. The time to get them, if they come from a corncrib, is August or September, before the mildew sets in. Or you can dry green cornshucks and spread them out on newspapers, but not in the sun. Put other newspapers over them. Put weights on those and let them dry out for four days. An alternative to that is spreading them out in the back of an automobile where it is dry. Once she has a good supply on hand, here is how Tennessean Jeanne Bowman makes her cornhusk dolls:

1. Soak some husks for 4 to 5 minutes until pliable. Drain them on paper or cloth.
2. Take a shuck about 6 inches long and lay it out flat. Then twist it in the middle until it is a bow-tie shape.
3. Lay a filbert or a hazelnut or an acorn with the cup off in one side of the "bow tie."
4. Fold the other half of the tie over it so that the nut is completely covered. The nut will make the head.
5. Tie the shuck with thread just under the nut. You will have a tail of shuck left. That's all right. You will use it soon.
6. Wrap a pipe cleaner in a shuck and tie it with thread at both ends. This will make the doll's arms.
7. Split the "tail piece" left under the head so that there are two tails at the front of the nut and two at the back. Slip the arms under the tailpiece and tie there with thread. You will still have pieces of tail left.
8. To make the bulk of the torso, take several strips of shuck about 6 inches long; lay them over the shoulders and cross them over the stomach.
9. For a bodice, take two pieces of nice, smooth, clean 6-inch shuck. Fold them lengthwise in the middle and lay them over the shoulders, too. Start at the waist and lay each over the shoulder on the opposite side. Tie these "tails" and the torso tails together around the waist with thread.
10. Now stand the doll up. Take eight shucks with the ends all facing in the same direction. Tie them around the doll's waist so that they are all facing upward — that is, covering her head.
11. Next, like peeling a banana, turn them down from her waist to make them into a skirt. Tie them at the bottom until the doll is dry. (A good place to dry her is on a cake rack, where there is ventilation underneath.) Don't dry in the sun or near a radiator.

12. When the doll is thoroughly dry, trim the skirt evenly so that the doll will stand.
13. Glue on corn silk or raffia for the hair (or, on a granny doll, you can use downy feathers, and paint on a face with acrylic).
14. For a simple bonnet, tear a strip of shuck about 1 inch wide and 6 inches long. Cross it in back of the head at the base of the neck and clip off all the excess except enough to be held in place by a strip of shuck used like a scarf, tied around the neck with a bit of thread.

A cornhusk granny doll carries an acorn basket.

A lobster claw, some unraveled string, and appropriate garb make a lobster witch to carry home from a Down East vacation. (Mark Lennihan)

a

b

c

d

e

(a) A pipe cleaner wrapped in shuck makes the doll's arms. (b) Several strips of shuck crossed over the stomach make the torso. (c) For the skirt, the shucks should be tied around the doll's waist, facing upward — over her head. (d) Peel them down, one by one, like a banana. (e) Smooth the skirt husks. Then tie them at the bottom.

12
Vacation scents

The sense of smell, it is said, triggers the memory more swiftly than any other sense. And woods and fields and swamps, of course, are filled with fragrances in summertime.

If you have been in the woods, pine or balsam needles, cedar bark, or sassafras root shavings can be stuffed into little pillows to perfume a bureau drawer. A combination of half sassafras and half rosemary with two pinches of orris root makes a nice dream pillow for a child's bed. Bayberries tied into a pretty cloth are excellent for waxing an iron.

If there are wild roses where you are holidaying, be sure to gather some for rose beads and potpourri.

ROSE BEADS

1. Collect rose petals. Sprinkle them with salt and run them through a meat grinder, using the very finest blade. Or you can pound them to a paste with a mortar and pestle, if you prefer.
2. Put the ground petals into an iron kettle or a bowl with an iron nail or some other piece of iron in it.
3. Each time you add more petals, regrind those you have just done with them. Soon the mixture will mold like clay and turn jet black.
4. Make beads of whatever size and shape you wish. Decorate them with fine lines. Set them aside on a screen or heavy tray in a warm, airy spot to dry.
5. When they are nearly dry, pierce them with a needle so you can string them. The needle should be large, for the hole will shrink. They may also be dried with a toothpick in them.
6. Return them to the drying area until they are thoroughly dry.

A Sachet, or Potpourri

1. Pick a variety of sweet-smelling flowers like honeysuckle, wild upland roses, bee balm, spicebush, and mimosa and spread them out on a couch or a rug to dry. (Their fragrance will perfume the room, too.)
2. Chop the petals fine or mix them in a blender.
3. Mix 1 quart of petals with 1 tablespoon of orris root in a jar. Close the jar and put it away until you are ready to make your sachets.
4. Then mix the petals and orris root in a bowl with 2 cups of kosher salt. If you like, add a few drops of oil of rose or oil of lavender or a tablespoon of allspice or cloves.
5. Put the mixture in 3-inch-square gingham bags. Tie or sew them at the top and they are ready to sweeten your drawer.

Pomanders

You've been on vacation in Florida and come back bearing citrus fruit. Lemons, limes, oranges, kumquats — all lend themselves to being turned into pomanders. Simply insert cloves into the peel close enough together so that no peel shows. Roll them in orris root or a blend of spices and orris root and let them dry for about four weeks.

Bayberry Candles

Barely fragrant when they are burning, but reminiscent, all the same, of a vacation outdoors, are bayberry candles. But beware — it takes about 20 quarts of bayberries to make two candles!

Cover the bayberries with water — barely — and let them simmer for 2 hours or so. Take them off the stove and let them cool. Skim the wax and berries off the top. Warm them a little. Strain the berries off and pour the wax into molds or dip a wick into it to make a candle.

13
Edible souvenirs

There is something irresistible about the powder blue of a blueberry hidden in green leaves, the gleam of a blackberry shiny in the morning dew. In the Southwest, purple prickly pears edge prickly pear cactus pads in the early summer and mesquite beans dangle from their trees. Wild strawberries nestle on grassy banks across the country when the Fourth of July arrives. As the summer progresses, elderberry umbrellas bob. Nuts thump onto the forest floor in October.

All these may be gathered for jellies or jams or wines, as a delicious winter reminder of your summer vacation. Of course, you must be sure that the fruit you pick is edible and that it is legal to gather it in a given state. But once these details are ascertained, pick away — though not to excess, for the birds, too, enjoy fresh berries, and unless the fruit is promptly used or frozen, it won't keep.

Persimmons are a favorite wild fruit in the hills of Tennessee. Sun-dried, they are known as Ozark dates. Here are two of Sara Shepard's persimmon recipes. She gathers the fruit near her home in Powell when it has fallen to the ground. As long as the fruit is not crushed, it will keep in a jar in the refrigerator for about three weeks.

OZARK DATES

Put a cookie sheet on the top of your car or on a tin roof. Lay the persimmons on it and leave them for a day or two (turning them once) until the seeds pop out partly. (They may also be put in a 150-degree oven overnight.) Cut the seeds out completely and cut the fruit into small pieces. Continue to dry the persimmons until all the moisture is gone. Pack them in sterilized jars and use them in any recipe that calls for dates.

142

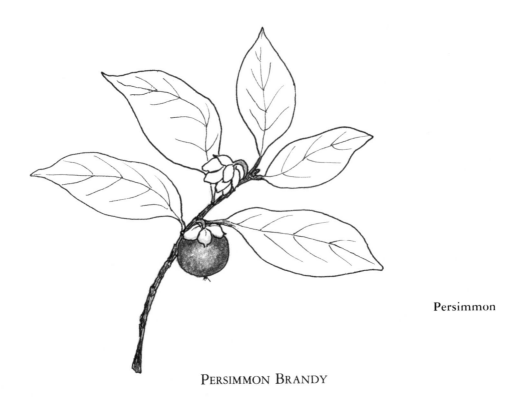

Persimmon

PERSIMMON BRANDY

Cover the bottom of a large, sterile jar such as a gallon mayonnaise jar with sugar. Work uncut ripe persimmons into the sugar. Be sure that they are covered with the sugar and add another layer. Work more sugar around those. Jam as many persimmons as possible into the jar, but be sure each time you add a new layer that you coat each persimmon thoroughly with sugar. Then cap the jar and put it on a shelf in your pantry. After a while, it will begin to liquefy and become persimmon syrup. In six months, it will be persimmon brandy.

WINE

In the southern mountains, wines of all sorts are made from the wild fruits. The following recipe is good for blackberries, strawberries, raspberries, wineberries, elderberries, muscadine grapes, or wildling peaches — any edible wild fruit that will ferment without going sour. Two good combinations are elderberry and blackberry, half and half, and choke cherry and wild plum. Beware of using elderberry alone, for it tends to be strong.

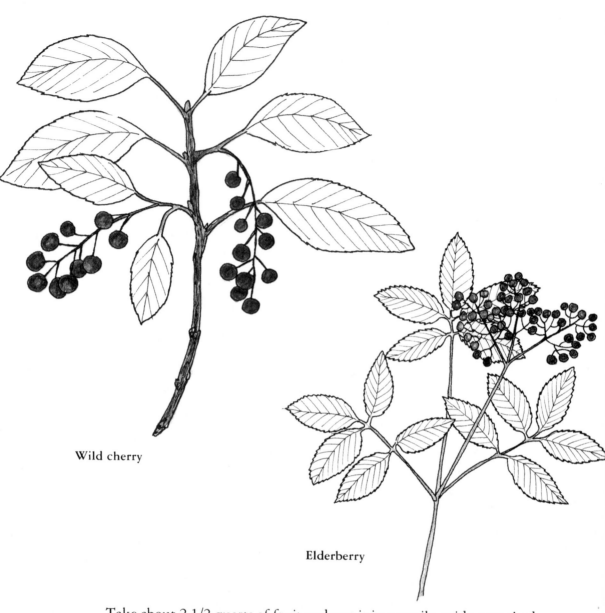

Wild cherry

Elderberry

Take about 2 1/2 quarts of fruit and put it in a sterile, wide-mouthed gallon jar. Fill the jar with fruit and water, using about half as much water as fruit. Cover the jar with several layers of cheesecloth or with cheesecloth with a saucer on top of it to hold it in place. Put a basin under it, for as it ferments it may spill over. Put the jar in a cool, dark place to ferment for six to nine days. During this time, occasionally mash the berries more into the liquid. At the end of the nine days, strain the juice and add 1 1/2 to 2 pounds of sugar for each gallon of juice. Pour the wine into a gallon jug with a small mouth. This time, fill the jar full. Even if the jar is full, you should have a little juice left over. Set this aside.

Every day, take the sediment that has gathered off the top of the jar with a piece of clean cheesecloth and add a little of the extra juice, but do not stir it. (If you run out of juice, just add water.) Continue this daily process until all the bubbling stops. Then clean out whatever sediment remains on the top and any fruitflies that may have gathered and close up the wine. Store it in a cool, dark place.

GRAPE JUICE

Grape juice is refreshing at any time of the year, and wild grapes abound in many areas. To prepare grape juice, simply puncture the skins of 2 cups of washed wild grapes. Put them into a sterile quart jar with 1/2 cup of sugar. Fill the jar with boiling water and seal and refrigerate it. Whenever you use it, strain it. (If you are in the South and use possum grapes, add another 1/4 cup of sugar to the recipe.)

Wild grape

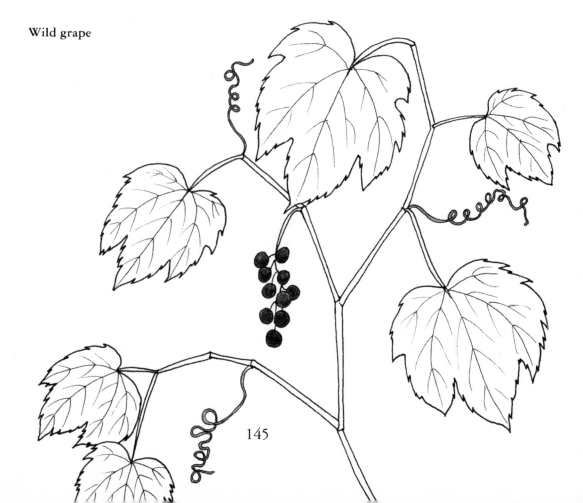

SASSAFRAS TEA

In the fall, when the sap is in the ground, and in the spring, when the leaves are just beginning to come out, are the best times for digging sassafras roots for tea. Let them dry for a week or two on a windowsill. Then chip the root into little pieces.

To make tea, take a handful of chips and put them into a kettle with 4 quarts of water. Let it boil until the tea is rosy, when it is ready to drink. If you would like a stronger tea, simply add more chips at the start.

SUMAC LEMONADE

The sumac that is good for picking is the staghorn kind, and you will know it by its upright red berries. Poison sumac grows in low, wet places and has drooping whitish berries. Do your picking for sumac lemonade when the berries are at their brightest, but never just after a rain or the tea will have no flavor. (Devotees explain that the coating that provides the flavor is washed off by rainwater.)

You will need a handful of berries for each quart of water you use. Either pour hot water onto the berries and let them steep until cool or simply put the berries in cold water in the refrigerator and leave them overnight. Sweeten to taste.

Sassafras

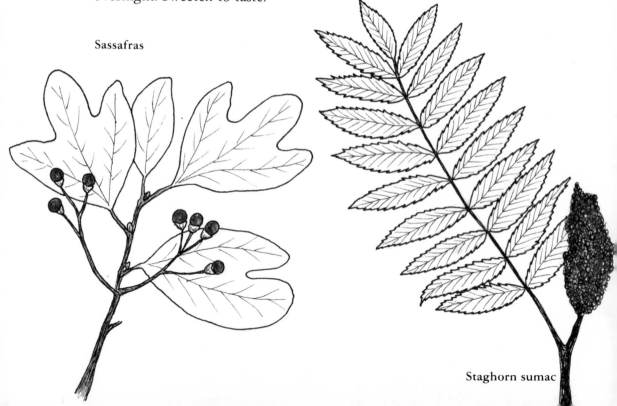

Staghorn sumac

Corncob Jelly

Should your vacation take you to farm country after the corn harvest, ask a farmer if you may have some corncobs from his crib. You can make corncob jelly with them. It doesn't matter if the corn is feeder corn, Indian corn, or a standard eating variety. All are equally good (though the prettiest jelly comes from the Indian corn, for some of its red color leaves the cob). For a good winter's supply of jelly, you will need twelve dried raw corncobs, 3 quarts of water, 1 package of Sure Jell, 3 cups of sugar, and 1 tablespoon of lemon juice.

Rinse the cobs well to rid them of the chaff that has probably remained after the corn was cut off. Break the cobs in half and boil them for about 30 minutes. Strain the juice through cheesecloth. When you measure it again, be sure that you have 3 cups. Add a little water if you are short. Add the Sure Jell and bring the mixture to a rolling boil. Add the lemon juice and sugar and bring to a boil again. Boil till it starts to jell on the spoon (probably about 1 minute). Pour into sterilized jars and seal with paraffin.

Rosa rugosa

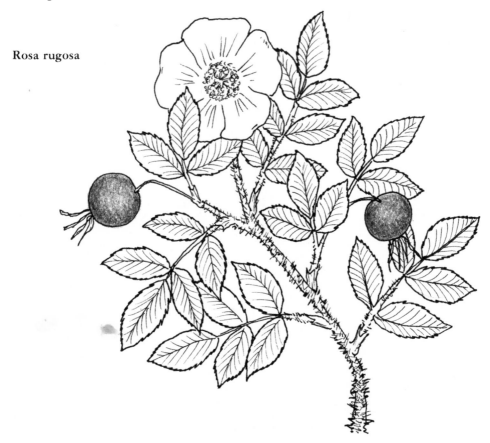

ROSE HIP JAM

All along the dunes and beaches of Cape Cod in late August and early September, the orange-red hips of wild roses — *Rosa rugosa* — brighten the seascape. Then it is time to go picking. Making rose hip jam is distinctly a rainy day operation, for it calls for plenty of time and patience to remove the seeds that fill the fruit of the wild beach roses. When you have gathered a goodly quantity of ripe and some unripe fruit, remove the stems and blossom ends and the seeds. Then cook the rose hips in water to cover until they are soft. Measure the pulp. Measure an equal amount of sugar, and cook the two slowly until they have the consistency of jam. A modern variation of this, offered by Louise Tate King of Martha's Vineyard, Massachusetts, cuts down considerably on the deseeding time by having you cook the fruit unseeded until tender; then put it through a Foley food mill and cook.

BEACH PLUM JELLY

A little later than rose hips, beach plums make their appearance in the same areas — dusty purple-blue fruit the size of a thumbnail. They are tart and not good to eat as they are, but their tartness in jellies and jams and conserves is a delicious accompaniment to meat, and many enjoy it, too, in a breakfast jelly. To make the jelly without adding pectin, combine 2 cups of ripe and unripe pitted beach plums with 2 cups of water and 1 cup of sugar, and bring the mixture to a boil. Boil hard for 1 minute, stirring constantly. Then simmer the mixture slowly for 45 minutes, or until it is like thin syrup. Drip the jelly through cheesecloth, but do not squeeze the cloth to accelerate the process or the jelly will cloud. (A variation on this, devised by Elizabeth Post Mirel on a Massachusetts holiday, is to pour the liquid jelly into a coffee filter paper and filter it for 1 hour. She incorporated this and many other beach plum recipes into a book called *Plum Crazy*). When all of the juice seems out of the jelly bag or filter, pour the jelly into sterile jars or glasses and seal with hot paraffin. For the first few hours, leave the jelly at room temperature, then refrigerate it. If it never achieves the spreading consistency you like, it may be boiled again for 30 seconds and then cooled again at room temperature.

If you don't want to go to the trouble of pitting beach plums, put them into a pot with a bit of water and boil them gently until all the pits are loose. Pour the mixture into a colander or a cheesecloth jelly bag and

Beach plum

Blackberry

let the juice drip through overnight. Add an equal amount of sugar to the juice you have and boil it until it sheets off the stirring spoon. Pour into sterile jars, top with paraffin, and seal.

Beach Plum Brandy

On a snowy midwinter night, it is pleasant to bring out the brandies and liqueurs after a dinner party. It is especially pleasant when guests exclaim over the pretty deep red liqueur and you explain that it is a product of your early fall vacation on Cape Cod or its offshore islands or Long Island.

Mrs. Vance Packard has devised a simple recipe that calls for combining 1 quart of plums, pricked, not quite 1 pound of loaf sugar, and 1/5 gallon of gin or vodka in a gallon jar. Cover it and leave it in a dark place for three months.

149

SPICED WILD GRAPE JELLY

For spiced wild grape jelly, you will need:

    4 quarts wild grapes
    1 pint vinegar
    1/4 cup whole cloves
    1/4 cup stick cinnamon cut into pieces
    3 pounds sugar

Crush the grapes; add the vinegar and spices and cook for 20 minutes. Add the sugar and cook till the juice sheets from the edge of your spoon or registers 220 degrees on a jelly thermometer. This makes twelve glasses of jelly.

BLACKBERRY AND APPLE JELLY

Down East in Maine, the blackberries in their thickets begin to ripen as summer ends, and just about the same time wild apples — knobby and green, but useful all the same — are forming. For blackberry and apple jelly, you need 4 quarts of apples to 2 quarts of blackberries.

Cut up the apples — skins, cores, seeds, and all — and put them, along with the berries, in a pot with enough water to cover. Boil the mixture for at least 20 minutes. Drip it through a cheesecloth bag overnight. In the morning, combine 1 cup of juice with 1 cup of sugar and boil it for about 20 minutes, or until it sheets from the edge of the spoon. Pour it into jelly glasses and seal with hot paraffin.

CRANBERRY JELLY

For the fall vacationer in many areas, there is a rich harvest — nuts in the woods, wild grapes on stone walls, wild cranberries in bogs in October and early November. If you boil 4 cups of cranberries in 1 cup of water and cook them for 20 minutes, rub them through a sieve, measure. Add 3/4 to 1 cup sugar to each cup sieved berries and cook for 5 minutes more, you should have a good wild cranberry jelly for Thanksgiving. It will be slightly more tart than a jelly made from commercially raised cranberries would be.

BLUEBERRY CONSERVE

Blueberries and huckleberries, their darker, more seedy, but more flavorful relative, are probably best in pies and next best dotting moist muffins. But if you want to take some away for a midwinter memory of Maine's Mount Desert Island or Blue Hill, it is simple to make conserve the way Mrs. Kenneth K. Stowell of Friendship does.

1 lemon
1 orange
1/2 pound seeded raisins
2 quarts blueberries
4 pounds sugar
1 cup chopped nuts

Put the lemon, orange, and raisins through the meat grinder. Add them to the blueberries and sugar. Boil gently for 45 minutes, or until mixture "jams" when cool. Add the chopped nuts. This is especially delicious with cold meats and Sunday morning pancakes, Mrs. Stowell advises.

WHITE SPRUCE TWIG BEER

If you go Down East in haying time, you will find white spruce twig beer a refreshment served down on the farm. But this refreshment keeps for winter enjoyment, too, if it is bottled and capped. This is how Mrs. Gertrude Hupper of Martinvale, Maine, makes it.

3 pounds loaf sugar
5 gallons water
1 yeast cake
1 small piece lemon peel
2 quarts spruce twigs steeped 1 hour in 1 pint boiling water

Mix all the ingredients together and put them in a crock. Cover it loosely, and set it to ferment in a warm, dark place. ("The old people," Mrs. Hupper says, "always set it behind the stove. Nowadays, I suppose you'd put it in the utility room.") When the mixture has fermented (in about a month), bottle it.

White spruce

SUN-DRIED WILD STRAWBERRY JAM

In Benzie County in northern Michigan, old-time strawberry jam was made by the following method with either wild or cultivated strawberries. Visitors there still enjoy it. Alice Nash gives these directions:

Put equal amounts of hulled strawberries and sugar, layer by layer, in a large kettle. Let the mixture stand overnight. In the morning, bring it slowly to a boil and simmer for 15 minutes. Pour it into shallow platters. Place glass (like window glass) over the platters and put them out in the sun for three or four days, turning the berries gently two times a day and bringing them in at night. At the end of the third or fourth day, the berries and sugar should be of the consistency of jam. Pour the mixture into sterilized jars and seal.

BLANCMANGE

Beachcombers who find the shores strewn with Irish moss can take some home in a plastic bag to make into old-fashioned blancmange pudding and top it with berries and sugar, beach plum jelly, or sliced bananas and cream. It needs such a topping, for it is a sugarless pudding.

> 1/2 cup Irish moss
> 3 cups milk
> 1/8 teaspoon salt
> 1 teaspoon vanilla

Soak the moss for 15 minutes in cold water. Pick out the discolored pieces. Add it to the milk and cook in a double boiler for 25 minutes. Strain. Add salt and flavoring and pour into individual molds. Chill. Unmold, and serve with sweetened fruit. This recipe serves five.

MESQUITE JELLY

For Southwestern vacationers, the desert, too, has native plants from which you can make edible souvenirs like mesquite jelly.

Genny Remington of the American Museum of Natural History's Southwest Research Station in Portal, Arizona, washes and breaks mesquite beans (picked in May or June, when the beans are green) into a large pot. She covers them with water and boils them for 30 minutes once the boiling has begun. Then she strains them and adds 1 cup of Sure-Jell

152

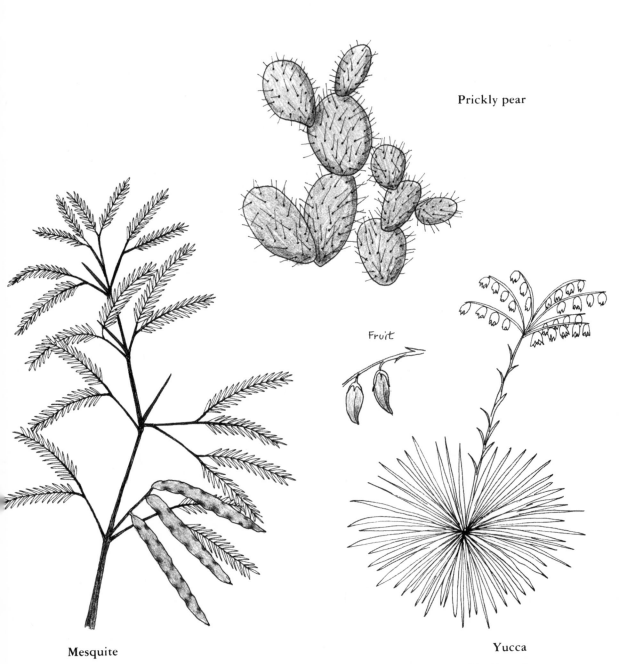

Prickly pear

Fruit

Mesquite

Yucca

pectin to every 5 cups of juice. She brings the mixture to a hard boil and adds 7 cups of sugar. She returns the jelly to a boil and boils it hard for 7 minutes. Then she skims it and ladles it into sterile jars.

The jelly she gets resembles apply jelly in color but may taste like cinnamon or lemon. Unfortunately, it could taste like soap (this depends on the mesquite beans you pick, and there is no way of telling in advance what the flavor will be), so taste the juice before you add the sugar and pectin to make sure you have a good kind.

PRICKLY PEAR JELLY

Also for Southwest travelers is prickly pear jelly, to be made in early summer when the prickly pears have turned purple. Like other desert products, be sure to have permission to pick from the owner of the land — and do your picking with kitchen tongs or some similar instrument, or the prickles will surely get you.

In picking, collect both ripe fruit and some unripe green pears. When you get back to your camp or cottage, spray-wash the fruit well in the sink or wash it outdoors with the hose — always handling it with the tongs. Put it in a large kettle and slice through it. Mrs. Remington, who supplied this recipe along with the mesquite jelly directions, says there should be sufficient water clinging to the fruit to cook it, but if not, a little might be added. Simmer the fruit for about 30 minutes, or until the juice starts to run, stirring from time to time. Then mash the fruit with a potato masher, continuing to cook it until you can mash all the fruit. Cook it slowly. Put the fruit into a jelly bag and let it drip overnight. In the morning, pour off the clear juice, being sure not to include any dregs.

Combine 2 1/2 cups of the cooked juice with one package of Sure-Jell. Never use liquid pectin. Stir constantly over high heat and bring to a fast boil. Add 3 tablespoons of lemon or lime juice and 3 1/2 cups of sugar. Return to the heat and bring to a hard boil, boiling for 3 minutes. Pour into seven or eight jelly glasses and seal with paraffin.

YUCCA CANDY

On the mesas and foothills of southern Arizona, in southeastern California, southwestern Colorado, southwestern Texas, and here and there in Nevada and Utah, the banana yucca grows, producing its banana-shaped fruit from May to September, depending on growing conditions. The fruit is reddish when it is ripe. That is the time to pick it and boil it for about 30 minutes. Drain and cool it. Remove the seeds and the peel and mash it. Then put it back in the cooking pot and continue to cook it until it is like jam. Sweeten it or not with honey, as you like. Spread it out on a cookie sheet and let it dry in a 200-degree oven (or in the sun). When it is dry, roll it into a sheet and cut off pieces as desired.

154

14
Mementos of your trip

Although most of the crafts in this book are made from natural materials, you needn't always select something wild as your vacation memory.

If you take a cruise or eat at exciting restaurants on your trip, you might bring home the menus and frame them attractively to decorate your kitchen walls. Or you can decoupage them onto a cylindrical object like a wastepaper basket.

WASTEPAPER BASKETS

One traveler who did this has an elegant wastepaper basket from a cruise aboard the Italian liner *Michelangelo.* A Sistine Chapel decoration by the artist served as the front of the menu. Several menus, combined, were just the right size to cover a wastepaper basket. A metal basket is best for this.

1. Cover the metal with decoupage medium (available at a crafts store).
2. Arrange the pictures.
3. Brush two more coats of decoupage medium on top and let dry.
4. Around the top and the bottom of the basket, glue on gold foil, grosgrain ribbon, or any pretty binding that will cover any mistakes in attaching the pictures.

POSTCARD BOXES

If you took a trip in the 1920s, the popular way to remember it was by bringing home postcards, punching holes in the sides about 1/3 inch apart, and lacing them together with colored ribbon into little boxes. Do the four sides first and then the bottom (and top, if you'd like one). Tie a bow at each corner and shellac them.

A modern version of this is simply to buy a decoupage box at any crafts store, sand and paint it, and decoupage postcards to its top and sides. If you use instant decoupage, you will probably need three to four coats, which can be applied in one day. You want to "sink the print" so you no longer feel any of the card's edges.

T-Shirts

Of course, with modern photographic processes, you can always have your favorite color photograph blown up and reprinted on a T-shirt. Most sophisticated photographic concerns will be able to do this for you or tell you where you can have it done. Or you could have a photograph blown up into a poster for your wall, or a black and white negative can be adhered to a silk screen.

Patchwork Quilt

If you travel abroad, why not pick up distinctive scenic handkerchiefs or ends of material that distinctly say to you where they originated. In England you could buy some Liberty print; in Finland, a little Marimekko fabric; in Thailand, a bright Thai print; in Hong Kong a bit of silk. And on it goes. Most countries have distinctive fabrics. Put together, they will make a delightful patchwork quilt.

Shadow Boxes

If you are simply a collector and not a craftsperson, put your seashells or horseshoe crabs or pottery shards from a Greek beach into a shadow box and label it. Whatever you gather, wherever you gather it, mark somewhere on it in indelible ink where you found it and the date. You'd be surprised how quickly you forget those specifics otherwise.

Gravestone and Brass Rubbings

In England between the thirteenth and eighteenth centuries, it was popular to lay a brass of lead, copper, and zinc alloy over a grave in a

Left: Menu covers from a cruise aboard the liner Michelangelo decorate a wastepaper basket. Right: Distinctive fabrics from your travels can become a patchwork quilt. Or you can make them into a "picture" and frame it.

This needlepoint footstool of her country house was stitched by Bettyanne Twigg.

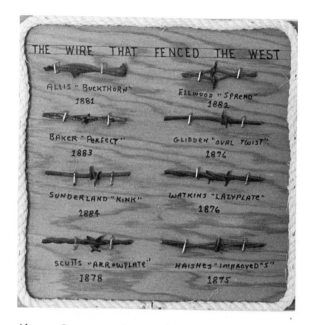

Above: On western vacations, many travelers collect barbed wire. They can be stapled to a piece of plywood and framed with rope. (David Dary)
Below: A coconut shell can be carved into a planter or cut into jewelry by an adept craftsman. (Alison Shaw)

Brass and tombstone rubbing is a fascinating hobby to pursue on your vacation. This one was done in Felbrigg Church in Norfolk, England, by Ruth Daniloff and now hangs in her Washington, D.C., home.

Buffalo and bison skulls may be found in remote areas of the western plains. This particular skull, found in northeastern Wyoming, was cleaned with a hose and dried in the sun for a week before being hung over a fireplace. (David Dary)

With decoupage medium, the wildflowers you pick can be pressed onto a plain parchment shade, then dried and sprayed with a clear acrylic spray. (Alison Shaw)

To press small wildflowers, lay them between clear Con-Tact and crepe paper. Put the "sandwich," flower side up, on several layers of Kleenex in a box. Cover it with sheeting and 1/4 inch of Flower Dri and weight it down with cardboard and books. Leave it to dry for three to four days. Remove the crepe paper backing and mount the flower arrangement on lightweight cardboard. This pressed flower picture is the work of Ruth Bogan.

159

church. Because its surface is raised, the design can readily be transferred to paper.

If you visit a church where you see brasses that appeal to you, ask if you are allowed to rub them. (Improperly done, the brass can be damaged, so some churches feel forced to forbid it.) If you receive permission, you will probably be told the best time of day to make the rubbing without interfering with church activity. Then either buy a rubbing kit or a cobbler's heel ball and a suitable piece of paper. It must, of course, be large enough to cover the brass. A heel ball is a form of wax and comes in various colors, so you may want a colored paper with a different colored wax or simply a combination of black and white. Rubbing kits can be bought in crafts supply stores in this country.

1. Clean the brass with a soft cloth to remove any dust or dirt that might scratch it when you lay down your paper and press on it. (Grit could also tear the paper.)
2. Lay the paper over the brass and attach it at the edges with weights and adhesive to keep it from moving.
3. With a clean cloth or your finger, find the outline of the brass and start rubbing. You will have to rub hard, but don't rub so hard that you do any damage to the brass.
4. When you are through, with a clean rag polish the rubbing before you remove it from the brass.

The technique is the same for rubbing tombstones — but beware especially of rubbing old slate tombstones, for they are easily damaged. Again, be sure to ask permission of the cemetery caretaker before starting your rubbing.

You can also rub the tops of manhole covers in cities on your travels. Many of them bear the name of the city and some decoration. Or there may be commemorative plaques on buildings that are worth rubbing and framing as trip souvenirs.

There are always the simple souvenirs like photograph albums and travel journals. These can be made ever so much more attractive if you buy the album or the journal where you are traveling and decorate its cover with something you pick up on those travels.

Whenever you go, wherever you go, happy vacation!

10/78

02